Praise for *Memorizing Scripture*

There are few disciplines Christians want to do more but actually do less than memorizing Scripture. Glenna's book is designed to help. It will motivate you to rediscover this important habit, instruct you on why it will benefit your life and faith, convince you it will foster your joy in the Lord, and help you build and maintain the practice. As we and so many other parents taught our children, it will help you to put the best thing (God's Word) in the best place (your heart) for the best reason (so you might not sin against Him).

TIM CHALLIES
Author of *Seasons of Sorrow*

Memorizing Scripture will be a resource I reach for and recommend often! It compelled me to know and love God through His Word, while equipping me with helpful tools to hide Scripture in my heart. Glenna Marshall offers us the principles with the practicals, exhortation with encouragement, and the truth with all the grace.

HUNTER BELESS
Founder of Journeywomen and author of *Read It, See It, Say It, Sing It: Knowing and Loving the Bible*

Muscle memory is an essential operation in our physicality. A thousand memorized micro-actions in exercise, cooking, texting, and driving help us flourish in everyday life. *Memorizing Scripture* by Glenna Marshall reminds us how vital Scripture memory is for our spirituality. You will enjoy this personal, inviting, practical, and invigorating work from Glenna. I trust it will encourage you to treasure Scripture as it did for me.

JEFF MEDDERS
Author of *Humble Calvinism*

For years, Glenna Marshall's faithful example of Scripture memorization has spurred me on to store up God's Word in my heart and mind, and this book is no exception. Glenna not only describes the fruit and benefits of memorizing Scripture but also provides practical methods and tips for even the most reluctant memorizer. This book will leave you encouraged and equipped to pursue a life saturated in God's Word—a life of wisdom, growth, and comfort in the Lord.

JOANNA KIMBREL
Content coordinator at The Gospel Coalition and author of *The Greatest Hero: The Book of Romans*

Authors sometimes write books about spiritual disciplines to help readers understand, books showing both our need for and God's command of such disciplines. And then there are those books that so tug your heart, so invite you in, so testify to the goodness of the discipline, that they make you want to participate in that discipline—like put the book down and participate right now. Glenna Marshall has written both books in one. Years ago, my memorization practice felt more vibrant, and *Memorizing Scripture* has given me the nudge to reengage a practice I've let get dusty.

BENJAMIN VRBICEK
Lead pastor at Community Evangelical Free Church in Harrisburg, Pennsylvania, managing editor for Gospel-Centered Discipleship, and author of several books

There is therefore now no condemnation for those who are in Christ Jesus. For the law of the Spirit of life has set you free in Christ Jesus from the law of sin and death. For God has done what the law, weakened by the flesh, could not do. By sending his own Son in the likeness of sinful flesh and for sin, he condemned sin in the flesh, in order that the righteous requirement of the law might be fulfilled in us, who walk not according to the flesh but according to the Spirit. For those who live according to the flesh set their minds on the things of the flesh, but those who live according to the Spirit set to

Memorizing Scripture

The Basics, Blessings, and Benefits of Meditating on God's Word

Glenna Marshall

be set free from its bondage to corruption and obtain the freedom of the glory of the children of God. For we know that the whole creation has been groaning together in the pains of childbirth until now. And not only the creation, but we ourselves, who have the first fruits of the Spirit, groan inwardly as we wait eagerly for adoption as sons, the redemption of our bodies. For in this hope we were saved. Now hope that is seen is not hope. For who hopes for what he sees? But if we hope for what we do not see, we wait for it with patience.

MOODY PUBLISHERS
CHICAGO

Edited by Pamela Joy Pugh
Interior design: Brandi Davis
Cover design: Faceout Studio, Molly von Borste
Cover white paper texture © 2023 by arigato/Shutterstock (195549638). All rights reserved.
Cover illustration of watercolor brush shape copyright © 2023 by Bankrx/ Shutterstock (2012855960). All rights reserved.

Library of Congress Cataloging-in-Publication Data

Names: Marshall, Glenna, author.
Title: Memorizing scripture : the basics, blessings, and benefits of meditating on God's word / Glenna Marshall.
Description: Chicago : Moody Publishers, [2023] | Includes bibliographical references. | Summary: "To love God with our hearts, we must first love Him with our minds. You will be transformed as the Bible takes root in your heart. We will-with the help of the Holy Spirit-be shaped like Jesus. You can do this! Memorizing Scripture shows you how!"-- Provided by publisher.
Identifiers: LCCN 2023002407 | ISBN 9780802431097 | ISBN 9780802473325 (ebook)
Subjects: LCSH: Bible--Memorizing. | BISAC: RELIGION / Christian Living / Spiritual Growth | RELIGION / Christian Living / Prayer
Classification: LCC BS617.7 .M36 2023 | DDC 220.07--dc23/eng/20230302
LC record available at https://lccn.loc.gov/2023002407

Originally delivered by fleets of horse-drawn wagons, the affordable paperbacks from D. L. Moody's publishing house resourced the church and served everyday people. Now, after more than 125 years of publishing and ministry, Moody Publishers' mission remains the same—even if our delivery systems have changed a bit. For more information on other books (and resources) created from a biblical perspective, go to www.moodypublishers.com or write to:

Moody Publishers
820 N. LaSalle Boulevard
Chicago, IL 60610

3 5 7 9 10 8 6 4

Printed in the United States of America

For my husband and my sons.

*Memorizing Scripture around the dinner table with you brings me
a lot of joy and makes me laugh harder than I probably should.*

*May the Word of God always taste so sweet to you.
"He-who-ha-ha."—Romans 8:32*

Contents

There is therefore now no condemnation for those who are in Christ Jesus. For the law of the Spirit of life has set you free in Christ Jesus from the law of sin and death. For God has done what the law, weakened by the flesh, could not do. By sending his own Son in the likeness of sinful flesh and for sin, he condemned sin in the flesh, in order that the righteous requirement of the law might be fulfilled in us, who walk not according to the flesh but according to the Spirit. For those who live according to the flesh set their minds on the things of the flesh but those who live according to the

---

introduction

The Long-Lost
Spiritual Discipline

*W*hen I was a child growing up in the '80s, my church participated in a Scripture memorization program designed to teach children to quickly memorize verses and the books of the Bible from Genesis to Revelation. At age six, I could locate any book of the Bible in three seconds or less, also telling you which books came before and after said book. I had about twenty-five verses stored away in my young mind for the competitions we entered with other churches. I'm sure the program was meant to teach children the value of memorization and to take advantage of their spongelike minds. I'll confess—the ability to locate books of the Bible in a couple of seconds has served me well to this day. But after graduating from the program somewhere around fourth grade, my foray into Scripture memorization came to a decisive end.

In my late thirties, I returned to Scripture memory for the first time since childhood—not for competition's sake but in desperation. The Lord had brought an area of besetting sin to my attention, and I was floundering in both disobedience and despair. Why couldn't I experience true victory? I was a faithful Bible reader and made time each day to pray. I was fully involved in church life as a pastor's wife and Bible study leader. Yet, the sin of anger was perpetually simmering beneath the surface of my thoughts, words, and actions. I felt stuck in a pattern of sin, guilt, confession, and repentance. *There must be some key to repentance that I'm missing*, I thought.

In frustration and fear that I would never have victory over my anger, I pleaded with God to help me see what I was missing. He brought to mind one of the verses I had memorized as a six-year-old in the Bible drill room of my little Baptist church. Psalm 119:11 says, "I have stored up your word in my heart, that I might not sin against you." The missing element in my fight against daily sin crystallized in that moment: hiding God's Word in my heart will help me not to sin.

This realization, a simple one really, sent me down a path of Scripture memorization that has transformed my mind and life. I began with a few verses, then a paragraph. I tackled some selected psalms, then the whole book of James, followed by Colossians, then 1 Peter. Scripture memorization became a daily spiritual discipline that has changed my thought life, encouraged me in despair, helped me stand firm against temptation, flowed into many gospel conversations, and given me what I need to say when seeking to comfort and exhort my church family.

As I've rolled the words of the Lord over and over in my mind, mumbling phrases time and again, I've thought deeply about their meaning, focusing on the context and intent in ways I have missed during daily Bible reading. While Scripture reading and study are daily disciplines I will hold on to for life, memorization has been a bridge between reading and living. It has moved me from study of God to affection for God. My only regret? That I didn't take the leap into the long-lost spiritual discipline of memorization sooner.

DO WE REALLY NEED ONE MORE THING?

I can almost hear what you're thinking. "You don't know me! I have the *worst* memory!" Or perhaps you feel there's just no more time in the day to do anything more. "Isn't reading my Bible enough? Do I really need *one more thing*?" I totally get that sentiment. Scripture memorization feels out of reach for many of us, like something we could never accomplish or commit to. But have you ever felt like you're floundering in the fight against a persistent area of sin? Have you wondered how to develop discernment or godly wisdom when you are surrounded with unbiblical influences? Do you freeze when trying to encourage someone or share the gospel, fumbling for the right words to say? Have you felt apathy toward the Lord and wondered how to rekindle your affection for Him? (Do you feel guilty for even admitting that last one?)

With the help of the Holy Spirit, Scripture memorization can shape the way you think and act and live. It can deepen your love for the Lord and provide the words you need in conversations with others. Hiding God's Word in your heart can help you walk a little more closely with the Lord who gave you His Word to equip you for everything you might need in this life.

But you're not going to memorize a verse or chapter or book in one day. Like our other spiritual disciplines, Scripture memory is not a race. It's a journey. It's not about recitation—it's about saturation. It can be done in tiny bits over long periods of time, yet yielding an immeasurable harvest of fruitfulness in your life.

Memorization can complement your daily Bible reading, helping you extract more from reading. The verses or chapter you're reading and studying will take on new depth and understanding as you recite them to yourself while you're cooking dinner or driving to work. The book your pastor is preaching through? Memorizing a key passage will help you engage more attentively to his sermons, which will resonate with you in a way you might have otherwise missed. As you fold laundry or wash dishes, mow the yard or take a lunch break at work, go for your morning walk or stand in line at the pharmacy—all these small moments in our days provide us with opportunities to think deeply and slowly about God's words. Something happens in our hearts when we heed the wisdom of meditating on His Word day and night (see Ps. 1:2).

Memorization moves us from study to application, from knowledge to affection. Rather than viewing Scripture memorization as one more thing on your spiritual discipline to-do list, you can view it as the continuation of what you're already doing.

Memorization might seem a lofty goal to you at this moment, but I can guarantee that as you work the practice of it into your daily life, you will see gradual changes in the way you think, respond, and feel. We will look at the basics and how-tos of memorization in this book, certainly, but we will also spend much time examining the blessings and benefits of applying what we've learned.

The Spirit will help you remember what you've worked to memorize, bringing it to mind during gospel conversations with your lost neighbor, or keeping it on the tip of your tongue while chatting with a hurting church member. The Word of the Lord is sharp, powerful, useful, corrective, and true. It will never return void. Whatever you pour into your mind will affect your thought life and influence your response to temptation.

When Jesus prayed for us in the garden of Gethsemane before His crucifixion, He prayed that the Father would "sanctify [us] in the truth" because God's Word is truth (see John 17:17). What sanctifies us—makes us more and more like Jesus—is God's Word. Scripture. All the words in the Bible. What goes into our hearts and minds should be what is true, honorable, just, pure, lovely, commendable, excellent, and praiseworthy (see Phil. 4:8). Only God's Word meets that description fully.

As you begin, little by little, to hide the Word in your heart, you will be equipped with the help of our faithful God to stand firm against temptation, discern what is true in a culture of lies, find deeper affection for Christ, and put off the old loves of your pre-converted life.

Why not take the leap into Scripture memorization? You have nothing to lose, for it is never a loss to think about God's Word. Whether it takes you a day or a year to memorize your first verse, your heart and mind will find rest and renewal as you begin to hide God's Word deep in your heart.

There is therefore now no condemnation for those who are in Christ Jesus. For the law of the Spirit of life has set you free in Christ Jesus from the law of sin and death. For God has done what the law, weakened by the flesh, could not do. By sending his own Son in the likeness of sinful flesh and for sin, he condemned sin in the flesh, in order that the righteous requirement of the law might be fulfilled in us who walk not according to the flesh but according to the Spirit. For those who live according to the flesh set their minds on the things of the flesh but those who live according to the

Know His Voice

Oh how I love your law! It is my meditation all the day.

PSALM 119:97

I was sitting in the aisle seat on a flight to Florida when I noticed the woman next to me reading the Bible on her phone. Psalms, I decided, after a closer look at the screen (I wasn't *trying* to snoop, but we were wedged in pretty tightly on that plane). Once she finished reading and slid her phone into her purse, I closed my novel and asked if she read her Bible often. "Every day," she replied. She looked to be in her seventies, and she told me that she worked in hospice care.

"What's your favorite Bible passage?" I asked her. Without missing a beat, she responded: "Psalm 23. That's what most of my patients want to hear before they pass away." I nodded. That was the first psalm I ever memorized and one I still call to mind when I'm dealing with fear or anxiety or insomnia (usually all three at once). It's a passage I'd want to be reminded of at the end of my life.

My seatmate told me that her Christian patients would often try to quote Psalm 23 with her as she read it, even if they hadn't spoken during the last days of their illness. The patients who didn't profess faith in Christ didn't seem to care whether or not she read Scripture, but she read it to them anyway. "The Christians, though," she told me, "know the Word and that's what gives them comfort before they die." I swallowed a knot in my throat as I pictured her dying patients quoting Psalm 23 with her. Christians know the Word because they know the One who spoke it. They know the Word Himself, and His voice comforts them in the valley of the shadow of death. And because they know His voice, they know that everything He has promised about eternity with Him will be true.

HIS VOICE, WRITTEN DOWN FOR US

Jesus talked about this vocal recognition in one of His parables. In John 10, He likened Himself to a shepherd and His people to sheep who follow Him because they know His voice. The sheep won't follow strangers whose voices they don't recognize. Jesus' parable teaches us that all who believe in Christ for salvation will recognize His voice. We know who our Good Shepherd is, and we do what He says because we know He is trustworthy.

The longer we walk with Christ, the more readily we'll recognize His voice. The more we listen to His voice, the more we'll trust it. And as we trust His Word, we'll be more confident to

stand firm on what we know to be true. Knowing His Word, rec-
ognizing His voice, exulting in our belonging to Christ helps us
discern what is true in a world that calls everything "truth." As
Jesus prayed, God's Word is truth. And by it we will be sanctified
(see John 17:17).

Listening to the voice of our Good Shepherd involves regular
exposure to His words. We have been
given an unimaginable gift in the complete, inerrant, eternal Word of God.
But more than just a book of words, the
Bible is God's voice, written down for us.
Through His chosen means of revelation,
we learn who He is, who we are, how we
needed rescue from slavery to sin and

> We'll memorize
> Scripture because it is
> no empty word for us
> but *our very life*.

the domain of darkness. We're given the story of Jesus' birth, life,
death, and resurrection—how He offers light and life to all who
believe in Him for the forgiveness of sins. We understand what it
means to follow Him, to persevere in the faith, to take the gospel
into the world, and to live as the body of Christ as we wait for His
return. We have the full story of redemption, and though we are
still living it, we know that God has written a very good ending.
He has given us what we need in Scripture to keep listening to His
voice until we see Him face-to-face. One day, we'll hear it with all
the glorious pitch, tenor, and tone that He intended—but until
then, we hold fast to the written word that was once a mystery
"but now revealed to his saints" (Col. 1:26). We'll read it, study it,
meditate on it, treasure it. We'll memorize it because it is no empty
word for us but *our very life* (see Deut. 32:47).

WHATEVER IS TRUE

In his letter to the Philippian church, Paul exhorts the believers to fill their minds with whatever is true, honorable, just, pure, lovely, commendable, excellent, and praiseworthy. He encourages them to continue holding fast to their faith in Christ by saturating their minds with true, good things. How do we know what is true? It's an age-old question, really. Philosophers have waxed eloquent and sometimes quite ridiculously about the origin of truth or whether it even exists. It seems that the longer human beings roam the earth, the more ludicrous our approaches to truth become.

In our twenty-first-century culture, whatever you believe can be "true" as long as you don't hold "your truth" over anyone else. As a result, we live in a society of people with a million different definitions of truth that clash horribly and crumble immediately beneath the test of time. Jen Oshman writes, "Here in the 2000s, we've successfully thrown off the shackles of any institutionalized definition of truth or reality or right and wrong. We've triumphed freedom as our highest good. Individual freedom trumps all former societal norms and values. It is ultimate."[1]

> We must think on God's truths and by them measure all that we see touted, advertised, and celebrated as true from the world.

American ideology these days touts that "*whatever* is true"—whatever you want to be true can be true *for you.*

---

1. Jen Oshman, *Enough about Me: Finding Lasting Joy in the Age of Self* (Wheaton, IL: Crossway, 2020), 33.

But Paul didn't mean "whatever" as in "choose what you want to be true." Paul meant "fill your mind with what is true." We already know from Jesus that God's Word is truth. His Word is also honorable, just, pure, lovely, commendable, excellent, and praiseworthy. We can and must think on these truths—God's truths—and by them measure all that we see touted, advertised, and celebrated as true from the world. We will be able to discern what is truly true by meditating on what is eternally true. And by meditating, I don't mean emptying your mind—I mean filling it up to the very brim.

MUMBLE, MUTTER, MEDITATE

Perhaps you're ready for me to give you a verse in Scripture that commands "thou shalt memorize Bible verses." You won't find it written quite that way, but the Bible is full of exhortations to treasure God's Word and think about it often. We'll explore many of these in the coming chapters, but for now, let's examine a few that leave no doubt as to how we fill our minds with whatever is true.

When God brought Israel into the promised land, He commanded them to be "careful to do according to all the law that Moses my servant commanded you. Do not turn from it to the right hand or to the left, that you may have good success wherever you go. This Book of the Law shall not depart from your mouth, but you shall meditate on it day and night, so that you may be careful to do according to all that is written in it" (Josh. 1:7–8). As a generation that had grown up wandering in the wilderness, the Israelites needed the guidance of the law to instruct them how to live as God's people in the land He would give them. Without the parameters of the law and the careful account of God's deliverance of their families from slavery in Egypt, Israel would run headlong into idolatrous worship like their pagan neighbors. Belonging to God meant living holy lives that reflected their Deliverer; thus, the people were to keep His words in mind at all times, meditating on them day and night so that they did not wander away from Him in disobedience. There was grave danger in departing from the commands of God, so the best way to hold fast was to keep His words ever before them.

We see similar language in Psalm 1 where the psalmist calls the happy, fruitful, blessed man one who delights in God's law, *meditating* on it day and night. The Hebrew word for "meditate" means to mumble or mutter aloud to oneself.[2] The way to delight in God's Word is to repeat it aloud to oneself, mumbling and reciting the words so that you believe them, live them, think them, practice them. In muttering the words of Scripture over and over again, we learn them, really *learn* them, because we think deeply on them in the mumbling repetition.

What protects the man in Psalm 1 from worldliness and sinful behavior? Meditating on God's Word day and night. What produces fruit in every season of life? Being rooted in God's Word, drawing nourishment from it at all times. This is more than daily Bible reading, though it is not less than that. It is an *extension* of Bible reading, really. Meditation plunges you deeper into the

---

2. "Lexicon :: Strong's H1897 - *hāgâ*," Blue Letter Bible, https://www.blueletter bible.org/lexicon/h1897/esv/wlc/0-1/.

verses and passages you're reading, saturating your heart with their meaning, one repeated word or phrase at a time.

In the New Testament, the idea of meditating on the Word of God is described as being immersed in Scripture. In Colossians 3:16, Paul tells the church in Colossae to "let the word of Christ dwell in you richly." Tim Keller writes that "meditation on the Bible is more than just intense thinking. . . . When Paul talks about the Word of God 'dwelling richly' within us (Col. 3:16), he is clearly talking of something beyond mere assent to information."[3] More is going on here than simply digesting knowledge or information. Because God's Word is powerful, it changes us as we think deeply about it. God's Word "is living and active, sharper than any two-edged sword, piercing to the division of soul and of spirit, of joints and of marrow, and discerning the thoughts and intentions of the heart" (Heb. 4:12).

> You'll never achieve any clarity or solid understanding of truth by emptying your mind and closing it down. Rather, you open up your mind and make it a house for God's words to live in.

I've had several surgeries to address a progressive disease that causes abnormal growths in my body, and I know how skillful a surgeon must be to remove what is diseased without compromising the organs. The scalpel must be sharp, the incisions and excisions

---

3. Tim Keller, *Prayer: Experiencing Intimacy with God* (New York: Penguin Books, 2014), 150.

exact. There is no room for error. God's Word is like that razor-sharp scalpel, and His Spirit works it in our hearts with precision like the most knowledgeable and practiced surgeon. His Word reveals sin that grows insidiously in the secret, hidden parts of our hearts. The more we dwell on His words, the more apparent the disease, and the more decisive its removal. What's left is a healthier Christian who can continue to grow and flourish in godliness as the Word of God dwells in him or her richly.

When the words of the Lord live in your heart, they change your heart. How do we let them dwell in our hearts richly? By feasting on them regularly, thinking on them, reciting them—mumbling them over and over to ourselves. Christian meditation is different from the world's poor version of it. You'll never achieve any clarity or solid understanding of truth by emptying your mind and closing it down. Rather, you open up your mind and make it a house for God's words to live in, where your thoughts are fed, rested, dressed, and wisely parented.

Old or New Testament, the exhortation for the people of God is the same: meditate on the words of the Lord so that you know His voice and know you belong to Him, so that you avoid sin, so that you stay the course of faithfulness and encourage other believers to do the same, so that your mind is transformed, so that you know what is true.

MEDITATE YES, BUT WHY MEMORIZE?

No one in the history of the church has had as much access to Scripture as we do in the twenty-first-century Western world.

As I sit at my dining room table in southern Missouri, there are seven Bibles I could reach in ten steps or less. Additionally, there's a smartphone, tablet, and a laptop in front of me, any of which I could tap, swipe, or command with my voice to open a Bible app, locate a website with multiple translations, or even read the Bible aloud to me right now. It's an embarrassment of riches, really. I can open a Bible anytime, anywhere. If anyone in history has ever *not* had to rely on their memory for what the Scriptures say, it's us. But this hasn't always been the case for God's people.

The saints of old were constrained by the expense and availability of papyrus or scrolls and ink, so memorization of the Torah was paramount to their knowledge of and obedience to it. As the New Testament books were written and circulated, they were copied and shared over time, but still—the early church did not have the physical access to printed Scripture that we have today. Listening to the Word proclaimed in corporate worship would have been their primary access to Scripture. To "let the word of Christ dwell richly" in a Christian with no written Bible would require them to remember the words of Christ that were taught in the church setting. Memorization of both the Old Testament and the emerging New Testament would have been deeply important for Christians to remain steadfast.

Consider our brothers and sisters in Christ today in settings where Bibles are illegal or where there is still no written language. How will Christians grow in

> **Why memorize now when we have such free access to the written words of God? Because God tells us to meditate on His Word *day and night*.**

the faith and remain steadfast under trial? The words must be memorized. I once read about incarcerated Chinese Christians who passed tiny strips of paper between their cells with verses of Scripture written on them. Once one prisoner had memorized the text, he would slip it to the person in the next cell.

In some countries where the gospel is being shared for the first time, the people group has no written language. Thus, missionaries must read the gospel story aloud often for the people to hear and remember until their language is developed in written form.

Or think back to the Reformation. One of the biggest problems in the Catholic Church of the sixteenth century was that the common person had no access to the Scriptures. The church had corrupted the Christian faith, requiring the purchase of indulgences for the forgiveness of sins, which the people would purchase in desperation, not knowing their money lined the pockets of the religious elite. Without access to the Scriptures, the people did not know what was true. They believed the lies of the leaders of the church because they did not know what God had actually said. They'd never heard His voice for themselves.

These examples might seem extreme. That's not us, right? We don't know what the future holds for us as far as religious liberty and our regular access to Scripture, but for now, we aren't held back from the Word by limited resources. Memorization might be important during times of illiteracy or oppression or poverty, but now? Why memorize now when we have such free access to the written words of God?

Lack of access isn't the only impetus for memorization. We memorize because God tells us to meditate on His Word *day and night*. So, how do we meditate? We *memorize*. John Piper says, "Unless you memorize Scripture you will not meditate on it day and night."[4] It's through memorization that we meditate, and it's through meditation that we memorize.

Psalm 119 is entirely devoted to the value of meditating on Scripture. Consisting of 176 verses that praise the benefits of treasuring God's Word at all times, each verse speaks of a specific blessing found in meditating on God's words. The psalmist uses several terms interchangeably for Scripture: law, precepts, rules, statutes, word, commandments, testimonies. These words represent the Torah, the first five books of the Old Testament, which the average Israelite most likely would have known from memory since the acrostic structure of Psalm 119 encouraged memorization. Below are some of the benefits and blessings of meditation on God's Word that the psalmist adulates in Psalm 119.

To endure suffering (vv. 25, 28, 50, 52, 54, 69, 71, 76, 92, 107, 114, 140, 147, 153, 165)

To avoid sin (vv. 11, 36, 101–102, 120, 128, 133, 176)

To seek holiness (vv. 9, 37, 80)

To remain steadfast (vv. 5, 33, 40, 149)

To know God (vv. 10, 12, 26, 68, 75, 137–38)

To have joy (vv. 14, 16, 35, 47, 56, 97, 111, 127, 143, 162, 174)

To gain understanding (vv. 18, 24, 27, 99–100, 104, 125, 130, 144, 169)

---

4. John Piper, "Meditate on the Word of the Lord Day and Night," Desiring God, January 3, 1999, https://www.desiringgod.org/messages/meditate-on-the-word-of-the-lord-day-and-night.

To be satisfied (vv. 19, 57, 72, 81, 103, 123, 131)

To discern truth (vv. 29, 43, 73, 105, 160)

To be vindicated (vv. 21–22, 31–32, 39, 51, 53, 82–88, 134, 154)

To obey God (vv. 34, 44, 55, 59–60, 62, 66–67)

To share God's Word (vv. 46, 74, 78–79, 136)

I don't know about you, but those promises, gifts, and encouragements are blessings I want for my own life as I follow Jesus each day. I want to know how to endure suffering, remain steadfast, and avoid sin. I want to know God better than I do so that I can love Him more and better grasp His love for me. I want to find deep satisfaction in the Lord and to have untarnished joy in Him when life is hard. I want to be vindicated from those who do not love what I believe, and I want the courage to share the gospel with them anyway. I want to know how to obey and be led by the Spirit to do so. Psalm 119 promises those benefits when we fix our minds on Scripture day and night.

No matter what century we live in, which country, or the level of access we have to the written Word, the biblical exhortations to meditate on Scripture still ring true for us. We must meditate on God's Word day and night, and in so doing we will flourish and grow in godliness and joy. Whether an Israelite on the banks of the Jordan, a new Christian in Colossae, or a believer living in Missouri in the twenty-first century, God's people must meditate on God's Word. He has instructed us to do so, and we must submit ourselves to His commands. As with all His commands, meditation is for our good and our joy. We'll spend the rest of this book examining *how* good and how joyous.

A WARNING AND A WELCOME

Any spiritual discipline can be performed in a legalistic manner. *Performed* is the key word here. The goal of Scripture memorization is not to wow your friends with recitations at dinner parties or to show off how spiritual you are at Bible study. If you've been convinced to begin memorizing Scripture at this point (I'll tell you how in the next chapter), be on guard now against any form of legalism in your heart. Memorization, while a sweet gift to help you grow in godliness, does not make you more loved by God. It will not curry favor for you with God as though you could perform in order to gain His approval. No, we already have all the love and approval we could ever need from God in Christ. We pray, read our Bibles, fellowship with the church, share the gospel, fast, give, serve, and yes—memorize Scripture—because we are *already* loved by God. Our spiritual disciplines help us to grow in awareness of that love.

As you stand guard against legalistic thinking, keep in mind that our goal in this book is to use memorization to help us stand firm on truth, saturate our minds with truth, comfort our hearts with truth, share truth, exhort with truth. As stated earlier, recitation isn't the goal, exactly. Saturation is. Andrew Davis writes:

> The point is not ultimately to be able to recite every verse perfectly, but to humbly and deeply saturate ourselves with the word of God. Regardless of what we eventually remember, the kind of meditation required for extended memorization will change us. That means no prayerful, meditative Scripture

memory is wasted, even if we seem to have forgotten it all (and you won't forget it all).[5]

Recitation might be a means by which we saturate, but it's the scriptural soaking that God uses to transform our hearts and renew our minds.

If you are a believer in Jesus, you already recognize His voice because you know Him. But now you can dwell on the sound and strength of His voice day and night through memorization. You don't have to finish this book before you begin. You can read chapters 2 and 3 for some practical tools that will help you get started with your first verse, chapter, or book. But stay with me as we look at how the practical parts of memorization begin to effect change in your daily life and conversations. It doesn't matter how old you are, how long you've been a Christian, how poor your memory, or how educated you might be. Scripture memorization is for every believer. You're welcome and encouraged to stand in a long line of saints who have beheld the treasure of Scripture and have spent their lives joyfully storing it in their hearts.

---

5. Andrew Davis, "Why I Memorize Books of the Bible," Desiring God, May 21, 2021, https://www.desiringgod.org/articles/why-i-memorize-books-of-the-bible.

memorization tip

Many of the Scripture writers used imagery to explain their points. Jesus often used parables, the poets used word pictures, and Paul used metaphors like armor and olive trees to explain abstract concepts. Pay attention to the word pictures used in Scripture and let the imagery help you memorize. For example, picture the tree planted by a river in Psalm 1. As you memorize, let the imagery fill your mind: tree planted, streams of water, leaf that doesn't wither. Notice the progression of sin in verse 1: walking, standing, sitting. The images were meant to help us both grasp the point and remember it.

suggested verses to memorize

Short form: Psalm 1:1–2, Psalm 19:7–11, John 10:2–3,
          Philippians 4:8
Long form: Psalm 1, Psalm 19, John 10, Philippians 4,
          Colossians 3

There is therefore now no condemnation for those who are in Christ Jesus. For the law of the Spirit of life has set you free in Christ Jesus from the law of sin and death. For God has done what the law, weakened by the flesh, could not do. By sending his own Son in the likeness of sinful flesh and for sin, he condemned sin in the flesh, in order that the righteous requirement of the law might be fulfilled in us, who walk not according to the flesh but according to the Spirit. For those who live according to the flesh set their minds on the things of the flesh, but those who live according to

---

chapter 2

You Can Memorize Scripture

I will meditate on your precepts and fix my eyes on your ways.

PSALM 119:15

I am not great at remembering names. Names are often the first thing we reveal to others about ourselves and the first thing to be forgotten. A social media meme said we're not actually so bad at remembering names. Rather, we're too self-focused to care enough about others to remember their names. Ouch!

I remembered that meme recently when I met a young woman at a conference where I was speaking. She was assigned to help run my book table, and while I know she told me her name, and I know I repeated it once back to her, I still promptly forgot it less than a minute later. I was too embarrassed to ask her again, so I just bumbled my way through our conversations for the weekend by avoiding calling her anything. For anyone who might have noticed my blunder, I certainly appeared to be too self-focused to bother remembering this sweet woman's name. And yet, I genuinely enjoyed my talks with her and wondered if the meme could be correct: Is it really true that we're just too self-centered to remember names? Or is it possible that we aren't using our brain's capacity to store new information?

When Scripture memorization first began to bear fruit and change my thought life, I shared the message of memorizing to anyone who would listen. I was a bit obnoxious about it, but I really did want other people to enjoy the benefits of hiding God's Word in their heart. Yet nearly every person I spoke with responded to my exhortations with the same words: "I could never do that. I have a terrible memory." Chances are, you've already had the same thought while reading this book. And perhaps my struggle to remember names resonates with you, solidifying your suspicion that you can't memorize Scripture. I'd like to push back on that. Because someone who has trouble remembering names shouldn't be able to memorize Scripture, and yet—*I can*. And you can too. It's not that you have a bad memory. It's that you haven't yet learned how to purposefully form new memories. Once you learn how to do that regularly, you'll be surprised at how well the brain God gave you works at retaining new information.

YES, YOU CAN

I used to think that remembering something depended on finding the information in the right spot of my brain where it was stored. If I could locate the file, then I could remember the information. But the brain doesn't work like a filing system. The brain works by connecting neural activity in patterns, using both information and lived experiences. We remember things by activating a solidified pattern of thoughts. We're not just *recalling* information; we're *replaying* it in our minds. And the more neural activity (think *details*) that's included in a pattern of thoughts, the more vividly we can recall the memory.

In her book on the brain and memory, neuroscientist Lisa Genova describes memory formulation in four stages: encoding, consolidation, storage, and retrieval.[1] I don't want to get too deep in the weeds of science here, but to help you understand that you can actually memorize not just a name but long passages of Scripture, humor me for a moment.

When you experience something, your brain takes in the experience through all your senses: sight, smell, sound, touch, taste. You know how you can smell someone's perfume or the aroma of food cooking and be transported to a memory from years ago? For example, every time I smell my husband's cologne on his shirts that I'm gathering up for laundry, I am suddenly a twenty-year-old college student on our first date together. I was nervous, excited, and

---

1. Lisa Genova, *Remember: The Science of Memory and the Art of Forgetting* (New York: Harmony Books, 2021), 16.

I was wearing gray pants and a navy shirt. The smell of Herrera can retrieve those memories instantly!

In addition to our senses, what we pay attention to in an experience helps our brains store information. What you purposefully notice is what your brain begins to encode into a memory. Then, your brain puts the information together into a pattern, consolidating many disparate details into one piece of information. There is even a part of your brain, the hippocampus, that works to consolidate all those different pieces of information into one memory.[2] Then your brain begins to store that information, moving it from the temporary holding place of your hippocampus to *multiple* locations in your brain. You retrieve the information by, in a sense, reliving the memory. So, the more details or things of notice that are attached to the memory, the more easily you can retrieve it.

> God designed your brain to store new information, and it can be helpful to understand how to use what God has given you to memorize His Word.

Why explain all of this in a book on Scripture memorization? I want you to see that God designed your brain to store new information, and it can be helpful to understand how to use what God has given you to memorize His Word. As in every part of living the Christian life, God has given us everything we need for life and godliness (see 2 Peter 1:3). He equips us for what He has called us

---

2. Genova, *Remember*, 16–17.

to. He designed your mind to memorize His Word. You may feel you have a poor memory, but you can memorize Scripture. What we pay attention to can be retrieved years after the fact, so if we consciously work to form long-term memories of Scripture, we can draw from them for years to come. The key here is consciously paying attention so that we form new memories. What we pay attention to while trying to memorize Scripture matters. The more details we bring into the experience of memorizing, the better our retrieval because the information will be stored in many parts of the brain, rather than that one hard-to-find file.

DIFFERENT BRAINS, DIFFERENT METHODS

In Deuteronomy 11, God commanded His people to keep His words before them constantly. He said to keep His words "in your heart and in your soul, and you shall bind them as a sign on your hand, and they shall be as frontlets between your eyes. You shall teach them to your children, talking of them when you are sitting in your house, and when you are walking by the way, and when you lie down, and when you rise" (Deut. 11:18–19). He also commands the Israelites to write His words on the gates and doorposts of their homes. They took this command quite literally, creating mezuzahs and phylacteries to store portions of the law of Moses on their houses and bodies.

While I don't think we have to go that far in obeying God's command to treasure His Word, I think the principle of keeping Scripture ever before our eyes stands true. God designed our brains, so He knew that we would need to meditate on His Word regularly in order to remember, treasure, and obey it. We can use many tools for thinking about Scripture, and those tools can serve as the means through which we write His words on our hearts and souls, binding them on our bodies, speaking of them wherever we go and to whomever we're spending time with.

Because God created us with unique minds, we differ in our learning styles. While I benefit from visual, kinesthetic, and auditory learning, writing something down increases my ability to retain information by leaps and bounds. Any kind of repetition, task association, or mnemonic device further entrenches new concepts or information in my long-term memory. The more help we give ourselves in retrieving the information, the more likely we are to remember what we've stored away.

> It's likely you'll work in methods from each category throughout your day to help you memorize a verse or passage.

Think of the many methods we have available to us as the mezuzahs and phylacteries: the writing of God's words on our hearts and souls, the practice of speaking His Word as we're walking by the way or with our families at home. Some of you remember things better when you hear them read aloud; others need to see it in print in order to retrieve it. But most of us could benefit from multiple methods of storing information when it comes to memorizing Scripture. To that end, I'm going to recommend *many* ways to memorize God's Word, and you may have to try several methods to see what works best for you. Leave a bookmark or two in this chapter and the next one so you can return to it for the recommended resources. It's likely you'll work in methods from each category throughout your day to help you memorize a verse or passage. The categories to follow all have some overlap and they often work together, so read through them all before choosing a couple to try.

Write the Word

Whatever method I choose to use in memorization, it usually begins with writing. Whether I put notecards with verses around the house or use my shower or dishwashing time for memorization, I have to begin by first writing the text. For some, the repetitive act of writing Scripture will be the primary means of memorization. If that's you, consider spending a portion of your Bible reading time simply copying the verses you're working on several times. Keep a spiral notebook or journal for that purpose. The simple act of writing the text can help with retention.

The first letter method has been the most useful tool for my own memorization work. Rather than writing out an entire text, simply write the first letter of each word in the passage. This takes far less time, and your brain can work faster at memorizing. For example, if you're memorizing Psalm 23, you would begin by writing this: *TLims; Isnw*. If you already know the first verse, it was probably easy to remember, "The Lord is my shepherd; I shall not want." You didn't really need *every* letter of *every* word; the first letter of each word was enough.

I have found the first letter method useful in reviewing large portions of the text. When I memorized the book of James (which took well over a year), I often reviewed whole chapters by writing the first letters of each word in a notebook. It might seem time-consuming, but the first letter method drastically cuts down on the time involved in writing the text while allowing the brain to go at the pace it prefers for reciting the text while writing.

Look at the Word

I love that God instructs us in the passage in Deuteronomy to keep the Word as frontlets between our eyes. We can keep Scripture before our eyes in many ways. Seeing it often helps us savor it. This might look like leaving your Bible out on the kitchen table, open to a passage you can read every time you walk through the kitchen. Or it might look like writing the text you're memorizing on notecards or post-it notes and leaving them around the house or office. I currently have Philippians 4:8 written in big letters on the door to our basement. Years ago, I painted the door with chalkboard paint for this reason, so when I want to work with my family on a verse, I write it on the door. Do you know how many times a day I see that door? Hundreds. If I make a point to stop and recite the verse even 25 percent of the times my eyes flit across it, I will have made great strides toward memorizing it.

> Pairing a daily task with memorization trains our minds to meditate on God's Word.

Along with the first letter method, my primary means of memorization is the shower method. Recommended by a friend years ago, this one simple practice has changed my life. Try this. Type and print out the text you want to memorize, then slide it upside down into a gallon-sized ziplock bag. Tape the ziplock bag (zipper side down) to the shower wall. Nearly every day, I spend a few minutes in the shower where I'm staring at Scripture while washing my hair. I have memorized whole books this way! I simply work on one new phrase or sentence every few days, reciting what I've already memorized before adding the new portion.

Pairing a daily task with memorization trains our minds to meditate on God's Word. When I step in the shower, my brain automatically picks up where I left off the previous day with memorization. You can do the same thing with almost any task. I keep a copy of the passage I'm working on taped to the window above the kitchen sink. Seeing it in the kitchen at each meal reminds me to work on it.

Bible memory apps are helpful tools to work different parts of your brain. While there are several different versions out there, I've come to appreciate the Verses app, as it incorporates multiple games for different learning styles. Verses uses the first letter method, word banks, speaking aloud, typing each word, and tap to reveal the text. There is also an option to create groups with others and have memorization challenges, and Verses will track your memory health so you can see how you've improved. Remember—giving yourself more options for forming a memory makes retrieval easier!

Listen to the Word

Auditory learners, you are especially equipped to lean into Scripture meditation in this day and age! The advent of audio Bible apps gives us plenty of opportunities to listen to the Bible being read to us. You can probably think of many times during the day when you can pop in some earbuds or let your vehicle's

Bluetooth sync with your smartphone, so why not let those times be used for listening to the words of the Lord? Or if you have a vision impairment, the audio Bible apps can be especially helpful as a memorization tool. While the brain does pretty much the same thing in transcribing information whether we read or listen to a text, the *process* of listening activates a different part of the brain than reading.[3] For that reason, it might help you pick up on the nuance of a phrase or items in a list in a passage of Scripture when you listen to it. Again, what we're doing in changing up our memorization tactics is giving our brains lots of paths to retrieve information.

> **Think of how many song lyrics you know by heart. Why were they so easy to memorize and why can you call them to mind right now? Music.**

Another way to listen to the Word is through music. I taught piano for nearly ten years, and I was always amazed at how many things the mind is doing at once while playing this instrument. While following a piece of music, the brain must read the music and translate notes to particular keys, use hand-eye coordination to strike the keys while reading the music, and pay attention to dynamics like speed and volume. Music actually *changes* the way we process information.

According to one medical journal, "listening to and performing music reactivates areas of the brain associated with memory,

---

3. Catharine Paddock, PhD, "Listening and Reading Evoke Almost Identical Brain Activity," *Medical News Today*, August 22, 2019, https://www.medicalnewstoday .com/articles/326140.

reasoning, speech, emotion, and reward. Two recent studies—one in the United States and the other in Japan—found that music doesn't just help us retrieve stored memories, it also helps us lay down new ones."[4] Music is such a powerful tool for forming memories! Think of how many song lyrics you know by heart. Why were they so easy to memorize and why can you call them to mind right now? Music.

You can find a list of resources at the back of this book, including whole albums that have helped me memorize certain psalms as well as some help for developing your own patterns of music for memorization. Singing the Scriptures is a great way to include others in your memorization process, especially children who aren't old enough to read yet. Before either of my sons learned to read, they could easily memorize song lyrics. We've learned that when we plug in Bible verses to familiar tunes, we give them a tool for memorizing words they can't yet read.

Speak the Word

Remember what we learned about biblical meditation in the last chapter? The term in the Old Testament for meditate means to mumble aloud to oneself. There's nothing like speaking the Word aloud to help you learn it. No matter what tools you use—audio apps, the first letter method, singing—recitation will be key in anchoring the text into your memory. Whether you're rehearsing

---

4. Dr. Anne Fabiny, "Music Can Boost Memory and Mood," Harvard Health Publishing, February 14, 2015, https://www.health.harvard.edu/mind-and-mood/music-can-boost-memory-and-mood.

your passages in front of the ziplock bags taped to the shower wall or writing out first letters in your notebook, speak or mumble the words aloud as you go. Don't just do it in your head. Say the words aloud. God gave us the command to meditate—to mumble aloud—for a reason. You won't get so distracted if you're using both your mind and your mouth. As you are filling your mind and heart with the truth of God's Word, the overflow from your lips will begin to effect change in your speech, habits, attitude, and relationships.

REMEMBER WHY WE REMEMBER

In our next chapter, we'll dig a little deeper into how to practically implement memorization tools into our daily lives, but I want to pause here and remind you why we're spending so much time on the *how* of Scripture memorization. The *why* matters more than the *how*. If you're a list-maker or a rule-follower or someone who simply likes to try new things, you might be tempted to jump into a method with little consideration for the reason behind it. Methods are tools, not rules. They help us retain Scripture, but the point of memorization is to grow in our love for Christ, to be able to recall His commandments and exhortations, to know what it means to follow Him, to have the language for encouragement or gospel sharing, and to be equipped to say no to sin and temptation.

We'll spend the bulk of this book learning the *why* behind memorization, but I want you to finish with the necessary tools to know *how* as well. Both are important, just as the Lord said all the way back in Deuteronomy. He wants us to speak His Word inside our homes and outside them, when we lie down and when we wake up. He knows that when we expose our minds to His words over and over, our hearts will be changed. The methods are the means by which we remember what He wants us to remember. And in remembering, our minds are transformed.

memorization tip

Pair your memory work with a daily task that you never skip. After a few weeks or months of doing this, you'll find that your mind automatically goes to the text you're memorizing while performing those daily rituals. You're training your brain to default to Scripture at different points of the day! What are some tasks you perform each day? Here are a few to get you started:

Taking a shower
Washing dishes
Preparing a meal
Folding laundry
Commuting to school or work
Brushing your teeth or doing your hair
Taking a walk or running on the treadmill
Eating a meal
Standing in line

suggested verses to memorize

Short form: Deuteronomy 11:18–19, Psalm 107:4–9,
        Matthew 22:36–40, Colossians 2:1–5
Long form: Deuteronomy 11, Psalm 107, Matthew 22:24–46,
        Colossians 2

---

chapter 3

How and When to Memorize Scripture

With my lips I declare all the rules of your mouth.

PSALM 119:13

When I was in college, I worked part-time as a dental assistant. One afternoon, a friend from church was in the office for a procedure, and when I stopped by her exam room to say hello, I noticed she was perusing a large binder with lots of plastic page protectors, sticky notes, and handwritten pages. I leaned closer and asked what she was working on. She held up her binder and said, "This is my Scripture memorization work." She walked me through the process she used to memorize Scripture with a friend, but even as she explained, I was surreptitiously backing out of the room. If I asked her any follow-up questions, I knew she would invite me into her process, and that was just not something I felt I had time or margin for.

Several months after that encounter, I ended up in a discipleship relationship with this woman, and you'd be impressed by how neatly (and how often) I skirted any conversation about memorization. I truly believed I didn't have what it took to memorize Scripture like she did, and I avoided the subject at all costs.

What I learned later is that though I didn't adopt her method, I too was able to hide God's Word in my heart during idle moments of my day. Looking back, I so admire my friend's dedication to memorizing Scripture in the cracks of her day! She was one of those women you knew was fully devoted to Christ by watching her life. She didn't memorize His Word because she was a legalist or a perfectionist. She loved the Lord and treasured His words enough to meditate on them in the dental chair. This was before smartphones or apps, but rather than bring a book with her, she dedicated her downtime to memorization. She had found a system that worked for her, and she used it often.

That is the principle I want you to take from this chapter: *find a system that works for you and use it often.*

In the last chapter, we discussed lots of methods and resources for memorizing Scripture. Now, we'll look at how to apply those methods on a regular basis, and we'll even get into some of the nitty-gritty patterns and helps for storing God's Word in your mind and heart.

THE POWER OF REPETITION

No matter what method you use for memorization—notecards, apps, the first letter method, writing or listening to the Word, or reciting it in the shower—repetition will be a necessary ingredient. Reciting, rewriting, remembering—what do all of these have in common? Repetition. Repetition turns the thoughts we're thinking into information we can retrieve again and again. Your brain was designed to remember things through repetition.

Lisa Genova refers to the process of holding whatever is in our minds *right now* as our "working memory" and that you use it "to keep a phone number or passcode in your consciousness just long enough to enter the numbers into your phone or computer before they vanish from your mind."[1] But our working memory wasn't designed to hold information for very long—only about fifteen to thirty seconds (which is a relief because how maddening would it be to keep everything you've ever learned or heard or observed in your working memory *for the rest of your life!* God designed us to forget things too). With repetition, though, you keep information in your working memory long enough for the hippocampus to consolidate the information into your longer-lasting memory.[2] If I had repeated the name of the woman at that conference every fifteen seconds for a minute or so, my working memory would have held on to her name, and as a result, I might be able to tell you her name today. Anything we want to remember, we must *re*member

---

1. Lisa Genova, *Remember: The Science of Memory and the Art of Forgetting* (New York: Harmony Books, 2021), 38, 39.
2. Ibid., 40.

or *re*think. Repetition aids us in moving a phrase or sentence from Scripture from the unknown to the well-known. Whatever method or combination of methods suit you best, they won't work without repetition.

> As you repeat and recite, you'll meditate on and think about the words.

So how do we harness the power of repetition for Scripture memorization? You'll use repetition to begin, practice, and finish memorizing a verse, passage, or book (yes, I said *book*. More on that in a moment). When you're standing in the shower in front of your ziplock bags of text, begin by reading and repeating the very first phrase aloud ten times. Then try to recite it without looking. Tomorrow, read the first phrase again and recite it ten times. When you've got it (and it may take a couple of days or a week), read and repeat the next phrase aloud ten times. Then recite it without looking. Then, circle back to the phrase you learned yesterday or last week and combine it with what you've just added. Read, recite, repeat.

While this part of memorization may feel rote, the purpose is to get the words down into the grooves of your mind and the corners of your heart. As you repeat and recite, you'll meditate on and think about the words. In his book on spiritual disciplines, Donald Whitney encourages changing up your emphases while reciting verses with repetition to help the meaning really sink in.[3]

---

3. Donald S. Whitney, *Spiritual Disciplines for the Christian Life* (Colorado Springs, CO: NavPress, 1991), 53.

For example, when reciting Psalm 23:1 multiple times, put your emphasis on the italicized words:

> *The* Lord is my shepherd; I shall not want.
> The *Lord* is my shepherd; I shall not want.
> The Lord *is* my shepherd; I shall not want.
> The Lord is *my* shepherd; I shall not want.
> The Lord is my *shepherd*; I shall not want.
> The Lord is my shepherd; *I* shall not want.
> The Lord is my shepherd; I *shall* not want.
> The Lord is my shepherd; I shall *not* want.
> The Lord is my shepherd; I shall not *want*.

I can attest to how helpful the use of emphases is with a repeated text; it's a tool I often use when dealing with anxiety and insomnia at night.[4] While my brain focuses on the meaning of the emphasized word in each repetition, my heart calms, feeling the depth of every word. The Lord watches over me, shepherding me. He gives me everything I need; there's no need for me to worry about the things I think He's withholding. He has rescued me from my greatest enemies of sin, Satan, and death through the work of Christ at the cross, so I can trust Him to provide for me in whatever situation I find myself, even anxious episodes in the middle of the night.

Do you see what's happening here? I'm not merely memorizing. I'm *meditating* on the truth of the words, and they are having

---

4. The use of repetition with changing emphases is also a tool recommended by my Christian counselor to whom I'm indebted for this practice that I can share with you.

their effect on me. I'm growing in love for my Shepherd with my mind and my heart because of the simple use of repetition. If you're listening to a chapter on repeat in the car or standing at the sink and working through the verses on the notecards propped up on your kitchen windowsill, use the same process. Read (or listen) ten times, recite ten times, repeat the process by adding a new phrase next time. The practices might seem pragmatic and rote, but they can result in your spiritual growth as you use them to love the Lord with your mind. Eventually, that love will warm your heart with affection for Him.

GETTING STARTED:
VERSES, CHAPTERS, OR BOOKS?

On her podcast, I heard Nancy DeMoss Wolgemuth share her experience of memorizing the book of Revelation.[5] *How is that even possible*? I wondered. Not long before that, I'd read *This Changes Everything* by Jaquelle Crowe with one of the teenaged girls in my church, and we both marveled at Jaquelle's story of memorizing the book of Romans with her dad. These are ordinary people doing something quite extraordinary. If they could do it, surely we could too.

This prompted me to move from memorizing a couple of verses to a whole psalm, then the first chapter of James, followed by the rest of James. Since then, though I do memorize verses or short

---

5. Nancy DeMoss Wolgemuth, "You Can Memorize More Than You Think," *Revive Our Hearts* podcast, 25:56, January 6, 2015, https://www.reviveourhearts .com/podcast/revive-our-hearts/you-can-memorize-more-you-think-1/.

passages from time to time, working through whole books of the Bible has been my preferred goal in memorization. Keep in mind—I routinely forget people's names. If I can memorize a book of the Bible, you can too. Let's look at why memorizing a whole book is important.

If you've done any in-depth Bible study in your life, chances are you've heard many Bible teachers or pastors praise the importance of context. Knowing the authorial intent and aim behind a book of Scripture helps us better understand the text and avoid twisting verses out of context to suit our desires or hopeful outcomes. To quote my pastor-husband, "The text means what it has always meant."[6] Understanding a verse in its greater context will make it more valuable and richer with meaning in our estimation when we see its place in a narrative, epistle, or Hebrew poetry.

The authors of the Bible, inspired by the Holy Spirit, were organized in their writings, and followed certain literary styles and rules. If you're memorizing the passage about the fruit of the Spirit in Galatians 6, it's helpful to understand that Paul was writing to Christians who were fusing works of the law with justification by faith, resulting in a false gospel. They could not expect to bear fruit of the Spirit through the works of the flesh because both our salvation and our sanctification are miraculous works of the Spirit. If you've meditated on Galatians 1 through 5, then chapter 6 packs more punch and makes more sense when you begin to memorize it. Context is key!

---

6. Special thanks to my husband, William, for driving this point home for his congregation. I have benefited greatly from his teaching on how to study the Bible.

In his booklet on memorizing large portions of Scripture, Andrew Davis writes:

> Memorizing individual verses tends to miss intervening verses that the individual does not feel are as significant. If we continue to focus only on our "favorite" passages of Scripture, we may well miss something new that God wants to say to the church through a neglected portion of His Word. God does not speak any word in vain, and there are no wasted passages of Scripture.[7]

Is memorizing a whole book of the Bible intimidating? Absolutely. But you do it the way you tackle any project that's overwhelming at first: bit by bit, a little each day.

This has been my experience with memorizing whole books. You don't miss anything, and those "favorite" verses will hold much deeper meaning when you've memorized them with the rest of the book in view.

Memorizing a whole book does beg the question: How often do you review an entire book when you've finished? Davis has a 100-day rule. After memorizing a book of Scripture, he advises reviewing it for 100 days before moving on to a new book of the Bible.[8] While I don't usually review a book for quite that long, I do find that at some

---

7. Andrew M. Davis, *An Approach to Extended Memorization of Scripture* (Greenville, SC: Ambassador International, 2014), ebook location 196.
8. Joe Carter and Andrew Davis, "Skip the Verse, Memorize the Book," The Gospel Coalition, May 13, 2014, https://www.thegospelcoalition.org/article/skip-the-verse-memorize/.

point I must consider a book finished and move on to the next because there is still so much more for me to learn. While I don't retain every single word I have memorized, I still have a good grasp on the flow and arguments from books I've memorized in the past, and many passages will stay with me for years to come. Just this morning while working on this chapter at the dining room table, my teenage son sat down next to me to read his Bible and eat breakfast. He showed me the verses in Colossians he was reading, and I surprised both of us by quoting the whole paragraph for him. I memorized that passage over a year ago! While I reviewed it monthly during the fifteen months it took me to memorize Colossians, it was encouraging to see that months of effort can bear fruit for the rest of my life.

Is memorizing a whole book of the Bible intimidating? Absolutely. But you do it the way you tackle any project that's overwhelming at first: bit by bit, a little each day. I recommend starting with a book like James or Colossians. They're not long books, and both have a flow that is relatively easy to follow. It usually takes me a year to memorize a book with four or five chapters. A longer book like Hebrews takes about twice as long. That's okay! The journey of memorization is where the benefits lie.

If a whole book still feels like too much, try a long chapter like Hebrews 11 or Romans 8. Or choose a psalm—many of them stand alone like individual books within the book of Psalms. If you make a goal to memorize ten verses this year, consider choosing ten consecutive verses from a chapter or psalm. It's perfectly fine to start with a verse you love, but I've learned that also memorizing the verses *surrounding* that favorite verse will enrich my understanding considerably!

Whatever you decide, first pray about a verse or passage that seems doable to you, and then go for it. Pick a date on the calendar and do try to finish by then—not because it's a race but because the goal might help you stick with the process. You'll be surprised what your brain can do with persistence and repetition. And if you need more accountability than a date on the calendar, try bringing others into your process.

MEMORIZING WITH OTHERS

During the early days of the COVID-19 pandemic, our church (like many) had to resort to Zoom calls for our services and Bible studies for a while. One of my friends from church had shared with me that she wanted to memorize Psalm 1. I offered to memorize it with her. We both worked on the six verses individually, and then recited them to each other on our weekly check-ins via FaceTime. One of our pastors decided to read Psalm 1 during an online worship service and asked us if we could share the screen on Zoom and recite the passage for the church. We each recited three verses, going back and forth until we finished the passage. While it was encouraging for the whole body to hear the Scriptures recited aloud, my friend and I were the ones who were truly blessed by the process. For a month, we had meditated on Psalm 1, studying the verses, delighting in them, and discussing them repeatedly together. We felt like flourishing trees planted by a river, perpetually nourished by the Word of God. The process of memorizing and holding one another accountable knitted our hearts together in spiritual friendship the way little else could.

I've memorized some verses and short passages with my children as well, and we've discovered that when it comes to hiding God's Word in the hearts of young kids, hand motions or rhythms are extremely helpful, especially if the kids are not old enough to read. A passage like Psalm 1 has many options for bringing the passage alive to young memorizers. The progression of sin in verse 1 (walking, standing, sitting) is easily acted out, and there are many ways to use hands and bodies to depict a tree planted by a river. While I typically save hand motions for memorizing with my kids, the motions are truly helpful if you're memorizing alone because you are giving your brain more neural pathways to retrieve that passage, as we discussed in the last chapter. We recently began memorizing Romans 8 as a family, and when one of Paul's lengthy sentences seemed difficult to wrap our mouths around, we set the sentence to a rhythm that our younger child pounds out on the dining room table. It helps every time.

> You could memorize with your roommate, small group, or even your whole congregation. The time you give to memorizing the Bible will never be wasted.

You don't have to be a parent to memorize with others. Remember my church friend in the dental chair? She met with a friend each week for the sole purpose of memorization. You could memorize with your roommate, small group, or even your whole congregation. A husband and wife could set a goal to memorize together, or a child could learn a passage with her grandparents.

We bring friends into our fitness and health goals with daily step challenges or recipe exchanges. Why not do the same for a practice that enriches and fortifies our souls? We all need a little extra accountability at times. Memorizing with others is a fantastic way to stay on track and share the experience and growth that comes from hiding God's Word in your heart.

MENTAL DOWNTIMES AND DAILY TASKS

One of the many excuses I used to give to avoid memorization was lack of time. We're busy people, and we're doing well if we can set aside some regular time for Bible reading and prayer, right? Who has time for memorization? You do! Memorization can easily be done in short bursts of time, so learn to use mental downtimes during your day. Sitting in a carpool line at your child's school? Whip out your notecards or listen to the passage you're working on in your audio Bible. Standing in line at the pharmacy? Play a couple of memorization games on your Verses app. Sitting in a waiting room? Keep a notepad and pen in your purse and write your passage a few times using the first letter method. If you're like me, you have several downtimes during your day, and you likely give it to the never-ending social media scroll. I often close my phone feeling restless and discontented. What a better use of my time and encouragement to my spirit to spend those mindless scrolling moments memorizing Scriptures about the Lord!

Are there times in your day when your hands are busy, but your mind is not? These are perfect opportunities for memorization! Consider daily tasks as an opportunity to "find time" to memorize. You're already folding laundry or commuting to work.

Incorporate some memorization into those moments. You don't have to find new time to memorize Scripture; simply redeem the time you already have. I promise that the time you give to memorizing the Bible will never be wasted.

A TYPICAL WEEK OF MEMORIZATION

While I will sprinkle in more practical applications of our memorization methods throughout the rest of this book, I want to walk you through the memorization habits of a regular person with a regular, unexceptional memory—me. Remember, I'm the woman who immediately forgot the name of the person she spent a whole weekend chatting with. My memory may not be great, but God made my brain, and He has given me what I need to meditate on His Word. He'll do the same for you.

I begin by choosing a book I've already studied so that the structure and purpose of the book are already pretty familiar. A couple of times a week, after my morning Bible reading and prayer time, I turn to a fresh page in my notebook and write out the passage of Scripture I'm working on memorizing, using the first letter method. Typically, I memorize a verse or two per week, which helps me get through a whole chapter in a couple of months. The first letter method allows you to move so quickly through a passage that this is a good time for a long review of a whole book or chapter you've been working on.

Later, after my morning walk and fixing breakfast for my family, I continue working on memorization when I take a shower, referring to the ziplock bags taped to my shower wall.

Sometimes I'll listen to the passage on repeat during my morning walk or while running errands. A few times a week, I run through the passage while working in the kitchen. Sometimes I recite it aloud to my husband on an evening walk to make sure I'm not skipping or forgetting parts. He can follow along on his phone and prod me when I get stuck. Often I recite at night when I cannot sleep.

"This Book of the Law shall not depart from your mouth, but you shall meditate on it day and night."

None of these are earth-shattering or paradigm-shifting practices. They're ordinary, repetitive parts of my days and weeks. Yet, they yield a harvest of fruitfulness, praise, love, and growth in my life because God is faithful to use our obedience for good. He is pleased for you to hide His words in your heart. He will use the time you give to memorization to bring about His good purposes in your life. When the Lord commissioned Joshua to take His people into the promised land, He commanded Joshua and the Israelites to obey all the words of His law, being careful not to turn away from them. He said, "This Book of the Law shall not depart from your mouth, but you shall meditate on it day and night, so that you may be careful to do according to all that is written in it" (Josh. 1:8). God then tells them to be strong—not afraid—reminding them that He would be always with them.

Keeping God's Word before us helps us obey Him. How can we obey God if we don't know what His commands are?

THE WHY REALLY IS IMPORTANT

Like Israel, we are a forgetful people, and we need regular exposure to Scripture to remember and obey. Memorization requires that we remember, recite, review. Thus, it is a vital tool God has given us to obey His Word and grow in love, faithfulness, and joy. Our aim is not the accumulation of words stored in our long-term memory. Our goal in Scripture memorization is to know our Lord more and more, which will result in a greater and deeper love for Him.

We've talked a lot about how to memorize Scripture, and I'll continue to give you some ideas throughout the rest of this book to help you form and retrieve memories of God's Word. As we move into the blessings of memorization in your daily life, I want you to see how the tools you implement today will benefit your spiritual growth for years to come. Memorization can feel like hard work because it *is* hard work, but the rewards are immeasurable and will aid you in your walk with Christ until you see Him face-to-face.

memorization tip

If memorizing with another person or group of people, try reciting a passage together, word by word. Let the first person say the first word of the passage, then the next person says the next word (and so forth), continuing in a clockwise circle until you get to the end of the passage. Start with a different person next time or move counterclockwise to change up who gets what word. My family frequently uses this tactic at the dinner table, and it usually results in a lot of laughter as well as memorization.

suggested verses to memorize

Short form: Joshua 1:8, Psalm 1, Galatians 6:22–23

Long form: Joshua 1:6–9, Galatians 6, Hebrews 11, Romans 8, James, Colossians

chapter 4

To Love Your God

You are good and do good; teach me your statutes.

PSALM 119:68

My husband and I recently celebrated our wedding anniversary. Sometimes I think back to our wedding day and remember how excited I was to marry the man I loved so much. And then I think, "I know I loved William, but I barely even *knew* him!" When I compare two years of dating and engagement with all these years of marriage, our love back in 2003 seems like a shallow, fragile affection that needed time to develop into real love. The years since spent knowing each other has made all the difference in our relationship. Love grows from familiarity. The longer I am married to William, the deeper and surer my love for him. It's not so much an exciting, frothy feeling as it is a weighty, well-rounded loyalty. We're not as giddy and overtly romantic as we were when we were first married, of course, but our years together haven't worn down our love for each other. Rather, the more we've studied one another, the stronger our love has become.

Marriage, even with all the flaws, sin problems, and imperfections that come with its participants, can help us understand how intimate relationships breed deep affection. You don't have to be married to get that, though. Think about your closest friendship or family relationship. The more you dwell on the other person and what might bring them joy, the more you want to bring that joy about. The more you seek to understand their personality, the more you love them for their quirks and enjoy the gifts they bring to the world. If we, in our human relationships, can find time and ways to deepen our affection for one another, how much more can we grow in our love for the Father who is unencumbered by bad habits, sinful displays, or annoying quirks? He is wholly loveable! Yet the way we grow in affection for Him isn't that different from the way we do that with other humans. Love grows from familiarity. And that's especially true when the Object of our familiarity is the definition of love itself.

LOVING GOD WITH YOUR MIND

Author Jared C. Wilson defines love as "an orientation toward others for their glory and for their good."[1] I think that definition

---

1. Jared C. Wilson, *Love Me Anyway: How God's Perfect Love Fills Our Deepest Longing* (Grand Rapids, MI: Baker Books, 2021), 31.

deconstructs the generic, ethereal idea of love we often have and distills it down to what it really is: affection that desires good for another. This is how God loves us. He loves us with our good in mind. God is love, and He demonstrated His love toward us in sending Jesus to die in our place for our sins. God authored and instigated the love in our relationship with Him, and our response should be one of love for both Him and His people (see 1 John 4:19–21). But we can't love the Lord without first knowing Him and His love for us.

We often think of our affection for the Lord like the effervescent feeling of a new romantic relationship. Sometimes we feel it, sometimes we don't. We want to love Him with our whole hearts, but sometimes we just don't *feel* anything. So, we surmise that something must be wrong or that we're in sin or that we're missing something. Any of those things could be true, yet Scripture teaches us that love for God isn't just relegated to the heart as we know it. Jesus summed up the greatest commandment saying this: "You shall love the Lord your God with all your heart and with all your soul and with all your mind" (Matt. 22:37). Love is more than a feeling. Loving God also has a cerebral aspect to it. We are to love God with every part of ourselves. If our hearts are lagging in felt affection, a renewed focus on knowing God will help us remember why He is the worthiest object of our love. To love God with all your heart, you must also love Him with your mind. Knowledge of God can grow your love for Him, and Scripture memorization is a beneficial tool for bridging the gap between knowledge and affection.

KNOWING AND LOVING GOD BETTER

In his iconic book *Knowing God*, J. I. Packer walks through the attributes of God's character as revealed in Scripture, asserting that knowledge of God must be grounded in God's own revelation of Himself in Scripture. In Romans 1, Paul says that "what can be known about God is plain to [people], because God has shown it to them. For his invisible attributes, namely, his eternal power and divine nature, have been clearly perceived, ever since the creation of the world, in the things that have been made" (vv. 19–20). That's what we call *general revelation*. We can look at creation and know there is a Creator.

But it is through God's specific revelation of Himself in Scripture, what we call *special revelation*, that we know who He is, that we have a sin problem, why He sent His Son, and what our response to the gospel call must be for salvation. God chose to reveal Himself through Scripture. As our Creator, He had every right to show us His character this way, so we must submit ourselves to *His* design for attaining knowledge of Him. If we want to know God, we must know Him in the way He has revealed Himself: Scripture.

> We need regular, persistent reminders of God and His character to discern what is true.

I hope you have a habit of Bible study that keeps you regularly examining the Word for truth about God and the big gospel narrative of Scripture. We won't know God or how to live as His people without regular time in His Word. And because we are habitually forgetful, we will be tempted to diminish aspects of His character when our circumstances loom large with suffering or difficulty. We'll forget that He loves us when we are lonely or sad. We'll begin to believe lies about both God and ourselves when temptation draws our hearts away from Him. We need regular, persistent reminders of God and His character to discern what is true.

Meditating on Scripture keeps God's faithfulness ever before our faces. The more we remind ourselves of who He is, the more we'll believe that *He is* who He says He is. And the more we grow in the knowledge of God, the more we'll love Him for being who He is. Knowledge in and of itself isn't the endgame here. As Packer encourages us, knowledge of God is the *means* to the end of loving and enjoying Him. He wrote:

> Our aim in studying the Godhead must be to know God himself better. Our concern must be to enlarge our acquaintance, not simply with the doctrine of God's attributes, but with the living God whose attributes they are. As he is the subject of our study, and our helper in it, so he must himself be the end of it. We must seek, in studying God, to be led to God. It was for this purpose that revelation was given, and it is to this use that we must put it.[2]

We never study God simply to acquire knowledge, and we don't memorize Scripture simply to be able to recite it. No, the bedrock of both study and meditation is relationship. We study and meditate on God's Word in order to know and love God better. Everything in our Christian life flows from what we believe

---

2. J. I. Packer, *Knowing God* (Downers Grove, IL: InterVarsity Press, 1973), 18.

and love about God. Meditation on God's chosen *means* of revelation helps us get there. Packer said,

> Meditation is the activity of calling to mind, and thinking over, and dwelling on, and applying to oneself, the various things that one knows about the works and ways and purposes and promises of God. It is an activity of holy thought, consciously performed in the presence of God, under the eye of God, by the help of God, as a means of communion with God. Its purpose is to clear one's mental and spiritual vision of God, and to let his truth make its full and proper impact on one's mind and heart.[3]

That impact that Packer speaks of encompasses many things: conviction, repentance, humility, praise, adoration, exultation, and *love* for the God who is drawing us into a more intimate relationship as our knowledge of Him grows. Our growing knowledge of God through memorization of His Word should have a "full and proper impact" on our hearts. And if it doesn't, keep mumbling His words aloud to yourself until it does.

BEING FILLED WITH THE KNOWLEDGE OF GOD

In Colossians 1, Paul prayed that the Colossian Christians would be filled with the knowledge of God, which would bring about the fruit of wisdom, endurance, joy, and holiness in their lives (see Col. 1:9–11). It is knowledge of God that drives our Christian living. We

---

3. Packer, *Knowing God*, 18–19.

can't do the latter without the former. When we think deeply
about God as we know Him in Scripture, the truths about His
character permeate our circumstances, correcting our skewed
views of suffering or sin and sustaining us when we're weary. Paul
goes on in Colossians 1 to give the Colossian church some truths
about Jesus to chew on. He describes Christ to them in a way that
would encourage their perseverance in the faith and deepen their
love and gratitude for Him. When I memorized this portion of
Colossians a few years ago, I could not move past this paragraph
for many weeks because of the hold that it had on my heart when
I began to slow down and meditate on each individual phrase.
Paul writes about Jesus this way:

> He is the image of the invisible God, the firstborn of all
> creation. For by him all things were created, in heaven and
> on earth, visible and invisible, whether thrones or dominions
> or rulers or authorities—all things were created through him
> and for him. And he is before all things, and in him all things
> hold together. And he is the head of the body, the church. He
> is the beginning, the firstborn from the dead, that in every-
> thing he might be preeminent. For in him all the fullness of
> God was pleased to dwell, and through him to reconcile to
> himself all things, whether on earth or in heaven, making
> peace by the blood of his cross. (Col. 1:15–20)

The weeks I spent memorizing this passage have been some of
the sweetest in my years of memorizing Scripture. Each morning,
as I worked on a phrase about Jesus, my mind was filled with the
knowledge of my Savior. I mumbled the words during household

tasks. On morning walks, I turned the words about Jesus over in my mind, dwelling on the knowledge that He is God, that He is uncreated and yet submitted Himself to death and resurrection to guarantee my own future resurrection.

During the season I worked on memorizing this passage, I fought a lot of fear and anxiety. I suffer from a couple of autoimmune diseases, and my health had taken a hard turn a few months prior. I struggled to feel safe in my own body. The Lord didn't seem keen on bringing about physical healing, and I found myself wondering if He was as good and faithful as I had believed Him to be. Colossians 1 became a balm to help me remember what was true about the Lord.

The phrase "in him all things hold together" became a motto for me when I worked through my fears. Neither this world nor my health were spinning off their axis in uncontrolled chaos. Things had not escalated out of the Lord's sovereign control. No, Jesus holds it all together—the planets in their orbit and me in my own small rotations and revolutions. He holds my life together. My existence is upheld by the strong, capable hands of my Savior. That was and still is so comforting! As a result, the knowledge of His perpetual universe-holding deepened my love for Him while I worked on this passage.

> Memorization solidified comforting truths about Jesus in my heart.

In the years since memorizing Colossians 1, I have kept that phrase "in him all things hold together" in my back pocket, returning to it time and again to remember what is true about life and the world and my circumstances. Because He is first in everything, one day I will be with Him in my own resurrected body, free from the troubles of this world forever.

Do you see how the simple process of meditation on Colossians 1 led to deepened affection for the Lord? I had looked at my poor health and doubted that God was who He said He was. But each time I returned to Colossians to work on memorization, my uncertainties evaporated before the truths about Christ. I would have been encouraged and built up by simply studying that passage for a day or two, but to dive into it, to saturate my mind with the knowledge of Jesus, to spend weeks there mumbling the words aloud to myself—memorization solidified those comforting truths about Jesus in my heart. I moved on from that passage with deeper love for Christ as well as a better understanding of His love and care for me. Time spent knowing the Father, the Son, and the Spirit in Scripture will lead to deeper affection for God and certainty of His love for us.

LOVE HIM ANYWAY

Jesus' command to love the Lord your God with all your heart, soul, mind, and strength isn't an arbitrary demand from a love-hungry God whose strength ebbs and flows with our waxing and waning affections. God doesn't *need* our love because He is self-sufficient in and of Himself. He's no Tinker Bell whose existence depends on our belief. Yet, we are commanded to love Him anyway. Why? Because loving Him with all our heart, soul, mind, and strength is unequivocally for our *good*. Orienting our hearts toward what glorifies God will, in turn, keep our hearts happy in Him. The more we think about Him and grow in affection for Him, the fuller our joy. This is how we were meant to be—joyful lovers of God. He knew before He created the universe that our hearts would be most satisfied when we are satisfied in *Him*. So He set eternity in our hearts to this end (see Eccl. 3:11). We were created to love and adore Him.

> Joy isn't found in loving ourselves. Joy lives in deepened affection for our God.

When Jesus spoke about abiding in His love in John 15, He connected abiding to obeying God's commandments. It seems odd to link obedience with love, and certainly, we don't obey God *to be* loved by Him. We obey because we *are already* loved by Him. But when we obey Him, walking in His ways, observing His commandments, we will be more certain of our already-loved position in Christ. Joy is found in obeying the commands of the Lord. The way we obey His commands is to meditate on His Word, studying them, thinking about them, obeying them—taking our cue from Psalm 119. In God's Word we learn who He is, and knowing Him changes us. We are our most satisfied, happiest, joyous selves when we are fixated on the good character of the Lord. Joy isn't found in loving ourselves. Joy lives in deepened affection for our God. Jesus explained that His purpose in speaking these things about obedience and love was so that His joy may be in us and that our joy may be *full* (see John 15:11). Fixing the gaze of your heart, soul, mind, and strength on your Maker will cultivate more affection for Him, even when you don't feel anything.

There have been many times in my thirty-plus years of walking with the Lord that I have not felt great affection for Him. I want to love Him, but sometimes my heart struggles to produce any feelings of love for Him. This is where meditating on Scripture benefits our lagging emotions. Fixing our gaze on the Lord will tell our hearts what is true. And our love—not the flimsy, ethereal feeling of love but the loyal commitment to God's glory kind of love—will put down roots that blossom with true, heart-satisfying affection. That kind of love far outlasts the fleeting feelings of new romantic attachments. When you don't feel anything for the Lord, perhaps because of a spiritual dry spell or unexplained apathy, *love Him anyway*. Love Him with your whole self as Jesus commanded because it is for your good. Loving Him is for your joy!

Here's how that might play out through Scripture memorization. The Bible overflows with passages about God's good character. You can just about turn the pages of your Bible at random to find a passage to memorize that will stir your affection for Him, but I'd like to recommend Psalm 145 as a place to begin.

> When your heart feels dull and dry, resist the urge to fill up the void with entertainment or noise. Go to Psalm 145 instead.

Written by David, Psalm 145 is a study of God's splendor and majesty. As you walk through the passage, you'll see David begin with statements about God's greatness before moving to the impact of that greatness on His people. This is exactly the kind of passage we need when we struggle to feel love for God. We need a happy collision of God's faithful character and our unfeeling hearts. As we mumble the phrases from Psalm 145, rehearsing the truths about God in our minds and through our lips, we'll begin to believe them. Remember, repetition is our friend because we are forgetful. God's command to meditate on His Word was purposeful. He knew we would forget what was true about Him. He knew we'd need to keep coming back to His Word for truth.

When your heart feels dull and dry, resist the urge to fill up the void with entertainment or noise. Lead your apathetic heart to Psalm 145 and fill up the emotional void with truth about the God you are striving to love with your whole self. Type or write out the psalm. Place it in spots around your home or office where you'll see it often. Go slowly as you memorize phrase by phrase:

> "Great is the LORD, and greatly to be praised, and his greatness is unsearchable" (v. 3). *Obey the command to meditate to infuse your soul with affection.*

> "On the glorious splendor of your majesty, and on your wondrous works, I will meditate" (v. 5). *Meditate! Make a list of the ways God has already worked in your life. Remember them. Thank Him for them. Look to the story of Scripture and note how God has loved you with an everlasting love by giving you new life in Christ. Remember this. Thank Him for it.*

> "The LORD is gracious and merciful, slow to anger and abounding in steadfast love" (v. 8). *Let the true words about God refresh the dusty corners of your heart. Take out a notebook and write the verses, underlining each attribute about God that you see. Memorization is more than mere recitation. Memorization is dwelling on God's Word, and letting it dwell in you.*

"The LORD is good to all, and his mercy is over all that he has made" (v. 9). *Listen to Shane and Shane's song "Psalm 145," and sing the words to the Lord, praying them until they take hold of your emotions.*

After you memorize the verses about God's greatness, keep moving through the psalm so that you see what His greatness means for you as one of His people. "The LORD upholds all who are falling and raises up all who are bowed down" (v. 14). "You open your hand; you satisfy the desire of every living thing" (v. 16). If God satisfies every living thing, then He knows what you need and will fill your heart with that much-needed loyal love for Him. Keep working through the rest of Psalm 145, reflecting on His kindness, His nearness, His promise to fulfill your desire to love Him. Again, go slowly. Take your time with this exercise. If your heart is cold, your affection might need lots of kindling. But as you warm your heart with regular meditation on God's Word, you will begin to feel a blaze of affection for Him. Maybe not overnight or in a month, but with time. And that loyal love will be built not on ethereal feelings that can ebb and flow with circumstances but on truth and intimate knowledge of the One who loves *you* without faltering.

memorization tip

When you work on verses or passages that highlight God's character, ask yourself what is true about God. When you work on verses or passages that are confusing, ask yourself the same question—even if God is not explicitly mentioned by name. He is always sovereignly at work, and whatever text you're hiding in your heart can point you to His good character. For example, in Psalm 103:20–22, we see several commands for all of the created world to obey the word of the Lord. What do we learn about God from these verses? God is the Creator of the universe, the only One worthy of worship and praise. He sovereignly rules, and it is right for His creation to obey His Word. Set in its greater context, we see God is known for His everlasting steadfast love, which means we can trust Him to rule justly and with holiness.

suggested verses to memorize

Short form: Psalm 103:15–22, Psalm 145:8–9, Ecclesiastes 3:11, John 15:1–5, Colossians 1:15–20

Long form: Psalm 103, Psalm 145, Ecclesiastes 3:1–15, John 15, Romans 1, Colossians 1, 1 John

There is therefore now no condemnation for those who are in Christ Jesus. For the law of the Spirit of life has set you free in Christ Jesus from the law of sin and death. For God has done what the law, weakened by the flesh, could not do. By sending his own Son in the likeness of sinful flesh and for sin, he condemned sin in the flesh, in order that the righteous requirement of the law might be fulfilled in us, who walk not according to the flesh but according to the Spirit. For those who live according to the flesh set their minds on the things of the flesh, but those who live according to the

chapter 5

To Hate Your Sin

I have stored up your word in my heart,
that I might not sin against you.

PSALM 119:11

*S*everal years ago, my husband noticed a strange weed growing in the flowerbed by our back door. The weed had a thicker stem than your average unwanted plant, and we made a note to cut it back the next time we got out the gardening tools.

We forgot about the weed, though, and at the end of autumn, we realized it wasn't a weed at all. It was a small tree—a tree with a slender trunk that now stood a couple of feet tall. We didn't have the proper tool to cut it back, so we planned to borrow a saw in the spring and take care of it once and for all. But spring came and went and for whatever reason we never got around to cutting it back.

The tree now towers over our house, and its branches push up against our roof. Its trunk has widened considerably, knocking some of the bricks from the patio out of place. We now need a professional tree trimmer to cut down our "weed tree," as we've come to call it, and we need a brick layer to repair the crumbling patio. I don't want to think about what the root system might be doing to the foundation of the house. This tree didn't grow twenty feet overnight. It started as a small, seemingly innocuous weed that should have been dug up the moment we noticed it. Instead, left unattended, it grew into a problem we couldn't control.

Many of us have areas of sin that stand tall and towering in our lives, and we don't understand how they got so out of control. We see the damage our sin patterns have caused in both ourselves and those we love, but we feel helpless to fight them now that they loom so large in our hearts. The weed tree by my back door began as a small seed; our struggle with sin can have a similar small beginning. James tells us that "each person is tempted when he is lured and enticed by his own desire. Then desire when it has conceived gives birth to sin, and sin when it is fully grown brings forth death" (James 1:14–15). Our desires for evil things can lead us down a sinful path, and sin always leads to death. Perhaps we don't see ourselves desiring *actual* evil things, but Jesus is clear that the sinful thoughts and desires in our hearts lead us to act in sinful ways. It begins inside and grows, working its way out into our words and actions. "But what comes out of the mouth proceeds from the heart, and this defiles a person. For out of the heart come evil thoughts, murder, adultery, sexual immorality, theft, false witness, slander. These are what defile a person" (Matt. 15:18–20).

No one falls into bed with a person other than their spouse and becomes a sudden, unintentional adulterer. No, the adultery began long ago when a fleeting thought wasn't held captive in obedience to Christ. It began when a flicker of attraction was entertained rather than snuffed out. It grew from thought to fantasy to conversation to relationship to full-fledged, acted-on adultery. But the truth is, it was adultery all along. Jesus said that lustful thinking was the same as adultery, and hatred in the heart was just as good as murder (see Matt. 5:21–30). When it comes to fighting our sin, we must address it in the place where it all begins: in our minds.

EVERY THOUGHT CAPTIVE

According to a *Newsweek* article, psychologists have determined that humans have around 6,000 thoughts per day.[1] I've barely scraped the surface in learning how the brain works, but I would argue that some of our thinking is quite purposeful, and some isn't. Some thoughts seem to come to us unbidden, triggered by circumstances, conversations, or things we see, hear, or read. We cannot control our environments, but even if we turned off all our devices and lived sheltered from news or movies or media, we would still struggle with sinful thought patterns because the problem with sin has been ours since Adam and Eve bit into the forbidden fruit in Eden. Sinful thoughts are certainly encouraged by

---

1. Jason Murdock, "Humans Have More Than 6,000 Thoughts Per Day, Psychologists Discover," *Newsweek*, July 15, 2020, https://www.newsweek.com/humans-6000-thoughts-every-day-1517963.

our culture in the shows we watch, the music we listen to, and the people we interact with, but our problem of sin is our own personal problem. The sin is inside us, as James pointed out; it's our own personal desires that are problematic.

> Real obedience to Christ must be from the heart. Therefore, our thoughts must be submitted to Christ in obedience.

Whether we are dealing with premeditated thoughts that are sinful or the kind that eventually lead to sinful thinking and living, we must do as the apostle Paul bids and "take every thought captive to obey Christ" (2 Cor. 10:5). Obedience to the Lord isn't merely external. Outward obedience is what Jesus often rebuked the Pharisees for because though they appeared moral or faithful to others, their hearts were like whitewashed tombs: clean and neat on the outside but corrupt and putrid with decay on the inside. Just as sin originates in the heart, obedience— real obedience to Christ—must be from the heart. Therefore, our thoughts must be submitted to Christ in obedience.

Taking them captive, as Paul words it, implies a mental battle, being ready to seize any thoughts that entice us to disobey God. This is a fight we are equipped to enter because every believer in Jesus has what she needs to stand firm against the attacks of our enemy, the devil. We have the gift of the Holy Spirit dwelling in us, and we have the weapons of warfare we need to say no to temptation.

Scripture is compared to a weapon in Ephesians 6. Paul calls it "the sword of the Spirit, which is the word of God" (Eph. 6:17), and it is both our defense and our offense against the fiery darts that the devil intends for evil in our lives. The Bible is the means by which the Holy Spirit helps us protect ourselves. With His help, we can wield the Word of God as a weapon against temptation so that we stand firm in the faith, take our thoughts captive, and submit them to the authority of Jesus. It's actually *from* Jesus that we learn how to do this.

DO BATTLE LIKE JESUS

Jesus is the only person to have walked this earth who never sinned. Maybe you're thinking, "Well, of course He didn't sin. He is God! But I'm a human. I can't say no to sin like He did." Jesus was, and is, God. But He also was human, and He wasn't indifferent to our struggles with sin. The author of Hebrews describes our Savior not as one who scoffs at our battle with ongoing sin but as one who *understands* it. "For we do not have a high priest who is unable to sympathize with our weaknesses, but one who in every respect has been tempted as we are, yet without sin" (Heb. 4:15). In the preceding verse, the author names that High Priest: Jesus, the Son of God. Our Savior knows what it means to be tempted by sin, and He sympathizes with our weaknesses. Though *He* stood firm every time, He doesn't hold our sin over us. No, He paid for it instead with His own blood at the cross. And because of that, we are encouraged to "draw near to the throne of grace, that we may receive mercy and find grace to help in time of need" (Heb. 4:16). We can cry out to Him for help in our moments of weakness because He has experienced temptation in every way and stood firm in obedience.

I've always found Jesus' temptation in the wilderness to be a strange but encouraging story. In Matthew 4, Satan tempts our hungry Savior, who had been fasting for forty days and nights in the desert. Physically, Jesus must have been quite depleted. The temptations of Satan to turn stones to bread, to avoid the suffering of the cross, to cast Himself off a building and watch the angels rescue Him—these temptations must have been somewhat appealing. Satan was poking where he thought Jesus was weak. His tricks are neither new nor inventive. He still pokes where we are weak. But Jesus did battle with Scripture that was embedded in His mind and heart. He replied to Satan's offers with Old Testament Scriptures, and He resisted the temptation to disobey His Father or deviate from His path to the cross.

> Jesus stood firm against Satan's tactics, and we can too when we have filled our minds with God's Word.

It's interesting to note that Satan also replied with Scripture, but his poor use of it was intended to manipulate Christ. We can learn from Satan's misuse of God's Word and Jesus' responses that the context of Scripture matters. We cannot twist God's Word to mean what it never meant when it was first written, even for memorization purposes. God's Word is not an incantation we can recite, hoping that it will make our wishes come true. It's living and active and has contexts of place and setting and original audiences that we must be mindful of, as we'll discuss in chapter 8. This is why memorization should be an overflow of the Scriptures we are studying or why we should consider meditating on larger passages. We want to be careful to understand the full intent and meaning as we use them to fight temptation or share the gospel or endure trials.

When we do battle like Jesus and fight temptation with Scripture, we don't want to only mimic His weapon of choice. We also want to wield it the way He did, honoring God's words in their proper context and use. Jesus stood firm against Satan's tactics, and we can too when we have filled our minds with God's Word. While we may meditate on Psalm 119:11 or Ephesians 6:17 in a moment of temptation, it can be helpful to study those verses in context when we memorize them. In a moment of weakness or doubt, we can recite Ephesians 6:17 while recalling that Scripture is a sword we wield with the help of the Spirit. We aren't fighting flesh and blood but the power and forces of the very enemy himself. We aren't weaponless or defenseless, and we aren't fighting alone. We have everything we need in Christ to stand firm. And that knowledge that we've meditated on and stored up in our hearts helps us take our thoughts captive so that we don't sin against God.

Jesus knows we are weak, and our struggles with sin don't have to alienate us from Him. Rather, they are prime opportunities to call out to Him for help and to bolster our faith with His very words. Dane Ortlund writes that Jesus "knows us to the uttermost, and he saves us to the uttermost, because his heart is drawn out to us in the uttermost. We cannot sin our way out of his tender care."[2]

---

2. Dane Ortlund, *Gentle and Lowly: The Heart of Christ for Sinners and Sufferers* (Wheaton, IL: Crossway, 2020), 83.

THIS IS YOUR WAY OUT

One Sunday at church, I experienced a sticky parenting issue that required a pretty serious discussion and disciplinary measure with one of my children whose offense was quite public. As both a pastor's wife and a mother, my pride was hurt, and having to react in public felt especially embarrassing. To be perfectly honest, I was just plain angry. Angry at my child for his disobedience and for doing it in front of others and angry at myself for not being the mother I wanted to be in that situation.

I walked my child to our car and prayed for help. I honestly wasn't sure how to handle this particular issue, and I was too frustrated—which is a path I usually follow toward anger. In this moment, the temptation to lash out in sharp words was strong. I started the engine and the Bluetooth in my van connected with my phone, kicking on the last thing I had listened to. It was my audio Bible app picking up where I'd left off on the way to church that morning. I was still memorizing the book of Colossians at the time, and the first verse that came over the speakers as I put the van in drive and left the parking lot was Colossians 3:21. With a child sobbing in the backseat, the first words I heard after praying for help in this moment of anger and frustration were this: "Fathers, do not provoke your children, lest they become discouraged."

This was a critical moment for me—a woman who struggles mightily with the besetting sin of anger. The words I was storing in my heart were not just coming to mind but were literally being played aloud for both me and my son to hear. I stopped the app and repeated the short verse a few times. It's written to fathers, but the principle applies to mothers as well. "Do not provoke your children." *What does provoking my son look like in this moment?* I wondered. *What would discourage him toward obedience?* I knew the answers immediately. Retaliating in sharp, needlessly angry words would both provoke and discourage him. Responding in sin would both provoke and discourage him. Blaming him for my hurt pride would both provoke and discourage him. When we arrived home, I sent him to his room so I could gather my thoughts. Chastened by the Lord, I prayed for His help. Loved by the Lord, I handled the situation with my child as best I could, provoking neither of us to anger or discouragement.

I wish I could say that all my parenting scenarios play out that way. I still struggle with the sin of anger more than I want to, but that day was a turning point in my fight against it. The Lord met me in my parenting and my weakness with His words, turning my mind and heart to meditate on Scripture. His words gave me pause, and in the pause, I could see the way out. In Christ, I was free to take it.

We are promised that our temptations are not only common, but they are also escapable. Paul wrote, "No temptation has overtaken you that is not common to man. God is faithful, and he will not let you be tempted beyond your ability, but with the temptation he will also provide the way of escape, that you may be able to endure it" (1 Cor. 10:13). When you have meditated on Scripture, the recollection of it might be the exit you're looking for in a moment of weakness. God is faithful, and He will give us a way out of temptation, for it is not His will for us to sin against Him. When we see the exit, we must remember that He is glorious and sin is death, so what is best for us when Satan tempts us to despair is to look at our Savior who understands us and run toward Him. *He* is the exit! Think on His promises, His beauty, His faithfulness, and run to Him.

When you are sitting alone in your home and feel the beckoning of the search engine or the TV show that's rated MA, Jesus is your exit. Return to the verses you've memorized about His sacrifice on the cross for the very sins your flesh wants you to enjoy. "For our sake he made him to be sin who knew no sin, so that in him we might become the righteousness of God" (2 Cor. 5:21). Jesus died to make you righteous. Flee from sexual immorality and run toward Jesus. Meditate on the way He paid for your sin at the cross by becoming your sin at the cross. This is your way out!

> At the end of a long day the temptation to devour every food that isn't nailed down feels strong. Food and drink are gifts from God, but they are poor masters and will never satisfy us. We belong to Christ.

At the end of a long day of work or parenting or loneliness, the temptation to devour every food that isn't nailed down feels strong. Maybe the bottle of wine in the fridge beckons for your attention more than it should. Before you give yourself to food or drink in a way that enslaves you, consider that you were made for more than this. Your body was made for Christ, not for chips or alcohol. You are not a slave to ice cream or merlot, not chocolate or iced coffees. Food and drink are gifts from God, but they are poor masters and will never satisfy us. We belong to Christ. When the fridge is calling or the drive-thru seems like the answer to a stressful day or an anxious night, meditate on this: "You are not your own, for you were bought with a price. So glorify God in your body" (1 Cor. 6:19b–20). This is your way out!

If you find yourself sitting at the coffee shop across from a friend, ready for a good dose of catch-up and conversation, what do you do with the small urge to bring up that mutual friend from church? Do you verbally dissect her and hedge your criticisms with, "I'm just concerned about her," or do you pause and look for the way out? Perhaps you've been memorizing Ephesians 4, or if the temptation to gossip is regularly a strong one, perhaps you should *start* memorizing Ephesians 4. Here is your way out: "[bear] with one another in love, eager to maintain the unity of the Spirit in the bond of peace" (Eph. 4:2b–3). You cannot bear with one another in love if you are dismembering one another over coffee. Run for the exit of grace and kindness! This is your way out.

THINK ON THESE THINGS

Our sinful desires start small and grow when left untended. When we fill our minds with Scripture throughout the day, we give ourselves something new to think about, something besides the images on the computer screen, the simmering anger beneath the surface, the chips in the pantry. Not each of those 6,000 daily thoughts *have* to take us down a sinful path. God has given us a way to capture the tiny seeds before they turn into trees that do damage to our homes. While much of our fight against sin is done in the moment as we remember God's Word and look for the way out, some of our work must be proactive and preparatory.

The work we do in daily memorization serves us later in critical moments of temptation. God's Word hidden in our hearts helps us see the exit much more quickly and clearly. You might feel that your daily memory work feels fruitless at times, but God will bring the verses you've labored over to mind when you need them most. He is faithful to help us in times of temptation, but He's also made it clear that Scripture is an important weapon we can wield as we flee sin and run toward Christ. Meditating on Scripture *today* might be the way out *tomorrow*. We can arm ourselves with Scripture when we're not tempted so that we're ready to stand firm when we are. The enemy is prowling around like a lion, looking for what he can devour. How do we stand firm without the words of the Lord to uphold us?

Some of our proactive work in fighting sin involves examining our influences. While we'll address this more in chapter 7, "To Renew Your Mind," the discussion of sin is a good place to consider what we regularly pour into our minds. What influences those 6,000 thoughts? Is it an endless stream of trashy shows? Or is it an Instagram feed that cultivates discontent in your heart? Maybe it's the music or podcasts you listen to while you exercise. Does it encourage you in holiness or does it breed complaints and irritation?

> As you stand at the sink and fight the temptation to fume over the pile of dishes you're washing alone *again*, turn your eyes to the Scripture passages taped above your sink.

While we must take action and turn off the TV, unfollow the

influencer, or unsubscribe from the playlist if those things lead us to sin, avoidance isn't the only tool we have to proactively fight against future sin. We're good at filling voids with other things, and sometimes the thing we choose to fill one formerly sinful void is just as sin-evoking as the first. Scripture memorization, however, can fill the void and turn our thoughts to Christ in the best way.

As you stand at the sink and fight the temptation to fume over the pile of dishes you're washing alone *again*, turn your eyes to the Scripture passages taped above your sink. Say them aloud as you scrub dishes. Turn the phrases over and over in your mind as you wipe down countertops. Attach memory work to your dish-washing so that in the future, your default response to this chore is thoughts of God. If on the drive home from work you know you'll be tempted to stop at your favorite store and spend money unwisely or hit the drive-thru for one of everything because your heart feels hungry, take a different route home and listen to your memory passages on audio. Say them aloud with the narrator and think on the riches of God's Word that are found in Christ. He satisfies like the richest of foods but *without regret*.

The more you meditate on God's Word, the uglier the weeds of sin will appear to you. You'll see the danger of letting them grow, and you'll be armed with what you need to uproot them from your life. We will always fight sin this side of heaven, but God has graciously provided us the truth with which to fill our hearts, reshape our desires, and renew our minds. As we grow in Christ, we'll become more aware of our sin, but we'll know that He is faithful to provide a way out. And by His grace, we'll be well equipped to run for the exit toward Jesus.

memorization tip

Think through the times of day when you are especially tempted to sin. Write out some verses on Post-it notes or index cards and place them in appropriate places to remind you of the truth when you need it. Or schedule a reminder to pop up on your phone with a verse to rehearse and recite. For example, if you are tempted with overindulgence or sinful content at the end of the day, meditate on Ephesians 6 or Romans 6, filling that aching void with truths that will help you wage war against temptation. Instead of mindlessly scrolling social media or streaming for something that your flesh hopes will lead to something more, open your Verses app and work on memorization with a friend who will check in with you for accountability. Or pray these passages until you go to sleep. Go to bed with no regrets.

suggested verses to memorize

Short form: Psalm 119:11, Matthew 15:19–20, Romans 6:12–14, Ephesians 6:10–18, Hebrews 4:15–16, James 1:14, 1 Corinthians 10:13

Long form: Matthew 5:21–30, Romans 6, Ephesians 6, James 1, Hebrews 4

There is therefore now no condemnation for those who are in Christ Jesus. For the law of the Spirit of life has set you free in Christ Jesus from the law of sin and death. For God has done what the law, weakened by the flesh, could not do. By sending his own Son in the likeness of sinful flesh and for sin, he condemned sin in the flesh, in order that the righteous requirement of the law might be fulfilled in us who walk not according to the flesh but according to the Spirit. For those who live according to the flesh set their minds on the things of the flesh and those who live according to the

---

chapter 6

To Remain Steadfast

This is my comfort in my affliction,
that your promise gives me life.

PSALM 119:50

A few months before my thirtieth birthday, my body turned on me. A sudden onset of back pain at night turned out to be a raging inflammatory disease I will live with for the rest of my life. One of the downsides of this autoimmune disorder is a little something called "brain fog." It's difficult to describe this phenomenon, but imagine your thoughts crawling through a big vat of honey. Your normal, quick neural activity seems to be dragging its way around your mind, often getting stuck for reasons you can't put your finger on. Some have described brain fog like the white snowy static you see on a television channel when the cable goes out. Or if you've ever seen a sloth do, well, *anything*—that's how you feel when fighting brain fog. We're moving at 0.25 the normal speed.

After years of ongoing health problems, I became ill with an infection that required massive rounds of antibiotics. As a result of the infection and treatment, my autoimmune disease kicked itself into overdrive and is still raging through my body as I write this a couple of years later. In addition to copious amounts of chronic pain, digestive disorders, sleeplessness, and anxiety, brain fog has been a fairly regular companion. Sometimes I open my computer and can't type a single sentence. A couple of months ago, I completely forgot my phone number while picking up a prescription at the pharmacy. I dozed off in the carpool line last week. I forget things constantly. My sluggish mind has made my attempts at Scripture memorization feel unbearably slow and fruitless. And yet, the slow plodding through Scripture retention—with brain fog and illness—has carried me through the last two years of physical suffering like nothing else.

WE ALL SUFFER

Elisabeth Elliot defined suffering as "having what you don't want or wanting what you don't have."[1] My mom has always shared the old adage—if we piled up our troubles on a big table and looked them all over, we'd each take home the troubles we walked in with.

---

1. Elisabeth Elliot, *Suffering Is Never for Nothing* (Nashville, TN: B&H Publishing Group, 2019), 9.

It does us no good to compare our sorrows or decide whose trial is better or worse to bear. We all suffer in this life, just as Jesus promised we would. He told us that in this world we *will* have trouble but to take heart because He has overcome the world (see John 16:33).

That's why I like Elisabeth Elliot's definition. After her husband was martyred in Ecuador in 1956, she shared the gospel liberally among the people responsible for his death, winning many of them to the Lord. Yet, she acknowledged that suffering encompasses more than the losses we experience through death. Suffering can include things like childlessness, undesired singleness, poverty, oppression, an unfriendly work environment, a broken relationship, church hurt, disease, miscarriage, and the list could go on and on. Many things cause us pain in this life. Indeed, even the *absence* of many things causes us pain in this life.

We're all touched by suffering, and yet for followers of Christ, we are called to steadfastness in our suffering. While that may seem as unattainable a goal as Scripture memorization seemed when you first opened this book, as with everything in the Christian life, God has equipped us to remain steadfast in faith in our suffering. Meditating on His Word is one of the gifts He has given us not just to survive suffering but to know He is carrying us through it.

THE BIBLE IS FOR THE SUFFERING

Have you ever noticed just how much of Scripture is dedicated to suffering? Some of our favorite passages sit against backdrops of bleak, dire circumstances. I've always loved the verses from

Lamentations about God's faithfulness and His mercies that seem to replicate anew every morning. Those verses have always been quoted to me as anchoring points of joy in the Christian life.

And yet, it wasn't until my pastors preached through the book of Lamentations a few years ago that I realized just how dark the night was for the people of God when the author penned the words. Jerusalem had been destroyed by Babylon, as God had warned, because Israel had continued in rebellion and idolatry. Now, in the ashes of captivity and loss, the words of Lamentations recount the griefs and sorrows felt in the wake of God's righteous judgment. But there, in come some of the most hope-filled words of Scripture: "But this I call to mind, and therefore I have hope. The steadfast love of the LORD never ceases; his mercies never come to an end; they are new every morning; great is your faithfulness" (Lam. 3:21–23).

Those words shine brighter with hope when we see the reason for their existence.[2] Deep suffering is the soil in which hope in the Lord grows. That is the gift of Scripture when life is falling apart. The Bible reminds us that hope is never lost if we are in Christ. The very reason we have the written Word of God is so that we don't lose hope in Him.

We may be shouting His Word in the night through gritted teeth or weeping with lament over our Bibles, but rehearsing Scripture gives us the language we need to endure suffering and remain steadfast through it. In his book on lament, Mark Vroegop writes:

---

2. I'm indebted to Mark Vroegop for his book on lament, which further shows how the passages devoted to suffering and lament are more than the sanitized verses we often see displayed on Instagram memes or coffee mugs.

God's Word says you can fight because you can call the promises of God to mind, and therefore, you can have hope. . . . We
interpret pain through the lens of God's character and his
ultimate mercy. By "calling to mind" important truths, we are
able to stop listening to the circumstances around us and even
the noise inside our heads. Lament dares us to hope again,
and again, and again.[3]

Scripture holds the promises we need to have hope in our suffering. So, filling our minds with it during the dark nights of the
soul will help us to remain steadfast in the storm. We can see our
suffering in its momentary nature when our eyes are fixed on the
promises of Christ's return and our home with God forever in
heaven. God gave us His Word—literally—to this end.

How do we hide God's Word in our hearts when we're suffering? Let me tell you how I've seen it done up close. My mom is the
best Bible studier I know. My childhood is marked by memories
of finding her sitting at the kitchen table reading her Bible in the
early hours of the morning. These days, when I visit my parents in
Tennessee, I still find her with her Bible open every morning. She
is a deep well of both knowledge of and affection for the Lord. I've
witnessed her love for Christ displayed in sacrificial care for countless people. She has housed college students and single moms in
her home, worked at a pregnancy care center for decades, taught
women's Bible studies, and served as caregiver to both of my grandmothers for many years. Her love for Scripture has infused her life

---

3. Mark Vroegop, *Dark Clouds, Deep Mercy: Discovering the Grace of Lament*
(Wheaton, IL: Crossway, 2019), 111–12.

with biblical love and service. It also has sustained her through suffering.

Not long after losing her own mother to Alzheimer's, my mom was diagnosed with a brain tumor. For the next several months, we walked through surgery and recovery with her. Prior to the surgery, I asked my mom if she was afraid. Strangely, she wasn't. Psalm 139:5 became her theme while she waited for the surgery date: "You hem me in, behind and before, and lay your hand upon me." I memorized it with her, and when I prayed with her before they rolled her back to the OR, I reminded her of the Lord's presence with her. I recited it while I waited for the surgeon to do his work. No matter what happened, her heart was safe with God because He had hemmed her in. I reminded my mom of this truth again many times when I stayed after surgery to take care of her.

> Even a single verse can sustain you when you are afraid, unable to think, or unsure how to pray.

One of the lingering effects of my mom's surgery manifested itself in an inability to gather her thoughts. Her mind just couldn't focus on anything very long. She battled aphasia for several months; words were difficult, and prayer was especially hard. I penned out some verses on index cards to place around her house. Psalm 139:5 was one of them. She held fast to 2 Timothy 1:7 as well, which she had memorized many years prior: "For God has not given us a spirit of fear, but of power and of love and of a sound mind" (NKJV). The inability to speak or hold a conversation was scary and unsettling. When her mind felt as *un*sound as humanly possible, she recited this verse repeatedly. It was, she later told me, *her lifeline.* Verses she'd hidden in her heart long ago served her when nothing else could, when she couldn't even remember how to pray.

With time, my mom recovered and returned to normal life; yet I learned during those scary months how even a single verse can sustain you when you are afraid, unable to think, or unsure how to pray. When your time is not your own, when your brain isn't functioning like you want, when you move from one season of suffering to the next, God's Word gives peace and certainty like nothing else.

The psalms are an excellent place in Scripture to work on memorization during difficult times. Many of the psalms are dedicated to expressions of fear, anxiety, and grief. But they don't leave us there. The psalmists point to God's faithfulness so that we can endure our trials. When we don't know what to pray, we can pray Scripture back to the Lord. Donald Whitney wrote that "God has inspired a psalm for every sigh," and explains that "the main reason why the psalms work so well in prayer is that the very purpose God put them in his Word to us is for us to put them in our words *to him*"[4] (emphasis added). Scripture memory won't end your suffering, but it can sustain you through it.

IF YOU'RE NOT SUFFERING NOW . . .

Don't worry, you will. You don't have to go out looking for trials. They will find you! Remember, Jesus promised that we would have difficulties in this life. But, if you're in a season of calm right

---

4. Donald S. Whitney, *Praying the Bible* (Wheaton, IL: Crossway, 2015), 54.

now, look at it as time to prepare for the future. Not in a "dooms-day prepper" kind of way, but in a wise preparedness kind of way. The memorization you're doing now will sustain you when you're going through a trial later. When pain wakes you in the night or you get the call that stops your heart with fear, the words you're burying in your heart today will blossom with comfort and minister to you then. Think of this as preemptive discipleship. You may not know what trial you'll face in the coming days or years, but the Lord does. And it is His will for you to not only survive it but to develop character and perseverance through it.

It's difficult to examine our suffering and quantify it as joy when we're in the middle of it, so now is the time to begin preparing your heart to be anchored in Christ when trials come. Romans 5:3–5 is a perfect passage to memorize now so that when suffering comes knocking at your door, you are ready not only to endure it but to embrace the sanctifying work the Lord will do in your heart through it. "Not only that, but we rejoice in our sufferings, knowing that suffering produces endurance, and endurance produces character, and character produces hope, and hope does not put us to shame, because God's love has been poured into our hearts through the Holy Spirit who has been given to us."

> He will never leave you and His Word will never fail you.

We don't have to be ashamed of the sufferings we endure as though we've done something wrong. If you are in Christ, Jesus took the punishment for all your sins so there's no condemnation for you any longer. Your suffering doesn't have to be a reason for shame. Rather, it can be a reason for hope. The Lord will see you through to the end! Paul tells us in Romans 5 that we can actually *rejoice* in our trials because God is using our suffering to produce endurance, character, and hope. We can endure because the Spirit lives in us and is with us in our suffering as an expression of God's deep and abiding love for us. James has a similar encouragement: "Count it all joy, my brothers, when you meet trials of various kinds, for you know that the testing of your faith produces steadfastness. And let steadfastness have its full effect, that you may be perfect and complete, lacking in nothing" (James 1:2–4). Whatever your "various trial" may be, God will not waste it. No, He will use it to shape your faith and cultivate faithfulness and perseverance in you. Your suffering will never be for nothing.

These are the reminders we need when we're hurting, so these are the truths we need to store up in our hearts for that day. Someone will disciple you through your suffering. Who is it? Will it be social media memes? Self-help, positive-thinking gurus with empty promises and hollow affirmations? Or will it be the unchanging, heart-steadying, inerrant Word of God? Let it be Him. He will never leave you and His Word will never fail you.

IF YOU ARE SUFFERING NOW

Maybe you're reading this and thinking, *I'm in the thick of it right now!* I'm with you. Before sitting down to write this chapter this morning, I had a doctor's appointment and left armed with a round of medication to alleviate yet another manifestation of my chronic disease, one that has the potential to permanently damage my vision. I only share this so that you know I mean it when I say that God's Word is a gift to you right now in the valley of the shadow of suffering. In the darkest nights of suffering, the promises of God's faithful presence and strength have carried me.

I always recommend 2 Corinthians 12 as a passage for meditation when I'm talking with someone who is living with pain or loss or perpetually deferred hopes. Paul was well-acquainted with suffering, so much so that he pled with God to remove his thorn in the flesh. When the Lord did not do as he'd hoped, Paul was still comforted by God's words to him, which gave purpose and meaning to his pain. Let this passage carry you through the dark nights of body and soul:

> Three times I pleaded with the Lord about this, that it should leave me. But he said to me, "My grace is sufficient for you, for my power is made perfect in weakness." Therefore I will boast all the more gladly of my weaknesses, insults, hardships, persecutions, and calamities. For when I am weak, then I am strong. (2 Cor. 12:8–10)

Maybe you can focus on only one phrase at a time. What I've learned in the years I've been memorizing Scripture is that every sentence can preach a sermon to your heart. If all you can do is breathe out one verse over and over again, by all means do it. Because my autoimmune disease is particularly painful at night, I've had to practice breathing through pain to stave off the accompanying anxiety. I do this with 2 Corinthians 12:9. Breathe in: "My grace is sufficient for you," and breathe out: "for my power is made perfect in weakness." Sometimes simply repeating that verse is all I can muster when the pain presses hard. But the promise of God's purpose in my pain stands true, even if I never see it with my own earthly eyes. When I am weak, then I am strong in *His* strength. He is at work in our trials.

If focusing on the purposes and sanctifying work of suffering feels like too much for you at this time, turn your attention to praying Scripture. The words will take root in your heart with meaning when you speak or write them to the Lord. And that is our goal here, isn't it? For God's Word to flourish in our hearts and shape our thoughts. We will be comforted more readily in suffering when our hearts have been planted with God's words to us in suffering. Hope will grow from the truths hidden in your heart.

Psalm 13 is well known for its honest lament to the Lord. I've lost count how many times I've penned the words of this psalm in my journals over the years. I've copied it enough times to engender a fair amount of memorization of the psalmist's deep-seated grief. The psalmist here—he *gets it*. God loved us in giving us Psalm 13. When you look at the brokenness of your circumstances, when you feel the knife-sharp edge of grief, when you can't get through the day without tears of longing and loneliness, call out with the psalmist:

How long, O LORD? Will you forget me forever?
How long will you hide your face from me?
How long must I take counsel in my soul
and have sorrow in my heart all the day?
How long shall my enemy be exalted over me?

Consider and answer me, O LORD my God;
light up my eyes, lest I sleep the sleep of death,
lest my enemy say, "I have prevailed over him,"
lest my foes rejoice because I am shaken.

But I have trusted in your steadfast love;
my heart shall rejoice in your salvation.
I will sing to the LORD,
because he has dealt bountifully with me.

The beauty of memorizing a psalm like this is that it not only gives you the language of lament and what Mark Vroegop calls *biblical complaint*,[5] it also gives you the language of continued faithfulness while in the midst of suffering. The Lord can handle your honest questions! He can listen with patience to your pleas for healing or the end of strife. He knows that you are weak and hurting. He *loves you* in your weakness and hurting. But you don't have to hunker down forever in your biblical complaints. You can, like the psalmist, move on to what you know to be true: the Lord is steadfast. He will not fail you, even now. Especially now. As you work to hide Psalm 13 in your heart while you're enduring a painful trial, pray it every time you are at a loss for words. Remember, God gave you His Word for this very purpose. Scripture is His gift to help you endure, and the Holy Spirit who lives in you will help you remember and apply the words you are meditating on, praying, crying, writing, and memorizing right now.

I don't know what kind of suffering you're piling up on the table right now. Chances are, if I examined it closely, I'd stick with what I've got. We all have thorns in the flesh that pierce and throb and remind us of the brokenness of sin in this world. Indeed, God has used my physical suffering and mental anguish to pull my heart

---

5. Mark Vroegop, *Dark Clouds, Deep Mercy,* 42–43.

toward eternity. As I've dragged my sluggish thoughts through passages like 2 Corinthians 12 and Romans 5, I am reminded that this life isn't all there is. One day we will enjoy new, resurrected bodies that will never shed a tear or experience pain. What a day of rejoicing that will be! But until then, we hold fast to the Word, which never fades and that carries us through every dark night of the body and soul. Scripture will help us remain steadfast.

---

memorization tip

If you are currently going through a season of suffering, now is a good time to practice praying God's Word, especially if you're struggling to know how to pray or can't stay focused. For example, pray through 1 Peter 1:1–9. As you pray the words to the Lord, focus on how He will use your trials to refine your faith, asking for Him to help you persevere. Try writing your prayer as you meditate on this passage. Pray through the passage every day for as long as you need it to carry you through your current trial.

suggested verses to memorize

Short form: Psalm 13:1, Psalm 139:5, Lamentations 3:21–23,
         John 16:33, Romans 5:3–5, 2 Corinthians 12:8–10,
         1 Timothy 1:6–7
Long form: Psalm 13, Psalm 34, Psalm 40, Psalm 77, Psalm 139,
         Romans 5, 2 Corinthians 12

There is therefore now no condemnation for those who are in Christ Jesus. For the law of the Spirit of life has set you free in Christ Jesus from the law of sin and death. For God has done what the law, weakened by the flesh, could not do. By sending his own Son in the likeness of sinful flesh and for sin, he condemned sin in the flesh, in order that the righteous requirement of the law might be fulfilled in us, who walk not according to the flesh but according to the Spirit. For those who live according to the flesh set their minds on the things of the flesh, but those who live according to the

To Renew Your Mind

Your testimonies are my delight; they are my counselors.

PSALM 119:24

*G*rowing up in West Tennessee, I went through a country music phase as did most of my peers. I love music that moves me, that tugs on my emotions, that tells a story—and country music definitely fit the bill during those moody, angsty teenage years. All you need is a broken romantic relationship and a twangy voice, and you've got the recipe for a hit country song. As much as I loved a good ballad about broken hearts, I noticed that all the mournful songs about regrets and lost loves weren't good for my seventeen-year-old heart. I felt perpetually gloomy, discouraged, and lonely. I was hyper-focused on not having a boyfriend when I should have been developing healthy friendships, working on college applications, and focusing on my relationship with the Lord. The music I filled my mind with on a daily basis affected the way I thought about my life, cultivating discontent and even some bitterness.

During that time, my family began attending a new church, and I was absorbed into a crowd of teenagers who loved the Lord and introduced me to all kinds of worship music and songs that contemplated life circumstances with the hope of the gospel in view. Listening to songs that exalted Christ and helped me think about singleness or loneliness through a biblical lens changed my thought life completely. What I began to pour into my mind turned my thoughts to Christ. And thinking about Christ throughout my day changed the way I reasoned, made decisions, spoke, and acted. What went into my mind came out through my words and deeds, but this time in a sanctifying way. I found it surprisingly easy to walk away from my stack of Garth Brooks albums for good.

In Matthew 12, Jesus explained that what is in our hearts will inevitably come out of our mouths. "For out of the abundance of the heart the mouth speaks" (v. 34). Remember all those 6,000 thoughts we have each day? Many of them will work their way out of our minds and into our words and actions. In other words, what we think about will come out in the way that we live. As believers in Christ, we must fill our minds with what pleases God so that what comes out will also please Him. We must give our minds what is true and good, because whatever it is that we spend time thinking about will influence our decision-making and actions. The apostle Paul had a phrase for this: renewal of your mind.

It's been a long time since I've indulged in country music, but there are other areas of my life that God is continually bringing to light for renewal. Invariably, the process of renewal must always begin in our minds. That's how we function as humans: influence > thought > action. Remember, James wrote about this when he explained how sin begins with desire in the mind and grows into full-fledged disobedience in action (see James 1:14–15).

As I have spent the last several years actively hiding God's Word in my heart, I've noticed a major shift in how I think, react, process, and respond to life circumstances. The more I dwell on Scripture, the less appealing I find the worldly offerings of entertainment and leisure. The more I mumble and meditate on the Bible, the less at home I feel on this earth. The more I roll around the good and true words of the Lord in my mouth and heart, the less I panic about decisions or difficult circumstances. While I expect the Lord will continue this heart-shaping process for the rest of my life, it has surprised me just how deep the work has been since adopting a regular habit of Scripture memorization. God's Word is rewiring my brain, so to speak. He is renewing my mind through the repeated, powerful words of Scripture. And my mind will never be the same.

GOD WANTS YOUR MIND

We have talked about the way the brain works in this book, and that might lead you to believe that mind renewal means employing brain exercises to stay sharp and stave off dementia. While brain health is important, crossword puzzles and sudoku aren't quite what we need for renewing our minds. Biblical mind renewal begins with infusing your mind with Scripture on a regular basis so that your patterns of thinking and living are shaped and influenced by what is always true, good, and praiseworthy. Scripture memorization is just the tool we need for renewing our minds!

If you've ever meditated on the book of Romans, you probably breathed a sigh of relief when you got to chapter 12. Paul shifts from the indicative (telling you who you are in Christ) to the imperative (telling you how to live in Christ). Those first eleven chapters are vital to understanding grace and justification through faith in Jesus. But what do we *do* with all that information? We get to chapter 12 looking for a call to action, and Paul gives us just that. He exhorts us to "present your bodies as a living sacrifice, holy and acceptable to God, which is your spiritual worship. Do not be conformed to this world, but be transformed by the renewal of your mind, that by testing you may discern what is the will of God, what is good and acceptable and perfect" (vv. 1b–2).

First, Paul tells us to consider our entire lives (not just Sunday mornings) as worship to God. That means everything we do and everything we are belongs to God. He has made us His own children through faith in Jesus. We are His. Our whole selves belong to Him, so our whole lives should glorify Him.

Second, as "living sacrifices" who belong wholly to God, we are to renew our minds so that we will be transformed more and more into the image of Christ. With what do we renew our minds? God's Word. Tony Merida explains that "this involves giving our minds to that which is good, right, and beautiful, not to what once marked our old way of thinking. It involves filling our minds with the truth of Scripture. . . . It involves meditating on the glory of God in Christ."[1] As we fill our minds, our actions are influenced first and foremost by God's Word. He wants all of us—not just an isolated portion of our week; not lip service. The Old Testament prophets did not speak favorably of people who honored God with their mouths but whose hearts—and actions—were far from Him (see Isa. 29:13).

From Genesis to Revelation, God is always after the hearts of His people—their whole hearts. He knows the difference between luke-warm acknowledgment of Him and wholehearted worship of Him. And He knows that we will only be satisfied and at peace when our whole hearts belong to Him. We can't hold back portions of our days from the Lord. Living your whole life, *coram Deo*, before the face of God, means that every nook and cranny of your day belongs to Christ. Thus, you must give your mind the scaffolding it needs to build your life around belonging to Him. According to Paul in Romans 12, wholehearted worship—being a living sacrifice—is inextricably tied to renewing your mind. We cannot renew our minds if we are not living our lives wholeheartedly

> There is no separation between sacred and secular in the Christian life. Even the way we decorate our homes or read books or pick out our clothing says something about Jesus if we belong to Him.

---

1. Tony Merida, *Christ-Centered Exposition: Exalting Christ in Romans* (Nashville, TN: B&H Publishing Group, 2021), 198.

for Him. We can't live wholeheartedly for Him if our minds aren't being renewed by His own words.

In other words, *God wants all of you.* He wants your mind, your heart, your obedience, your gifts. And it is in your best interest for all of you to belong to Him for that is where joy and peace will be multiplied to you. There is no separation between sacred and secular in the Christian life, and you'll only ever find soul satisfaction when you belong to the Lord wholeheartedly. He cares about how we spend our time and our money. He cares about what shows we watch and how we respond to current events or cultural crises. Even the way we decorate our homes or read books or pick out our clothing says something about Jesus if we belong to Him. Living wholeheartedly for Christ *is* worship. Renewing our minds with Scripture each day enables us to live fully devoted to Him—heart, soul, mind, strength. What's more, renewing our mind by dwelling on Scripture helps us to *want* to live that way.

You are already renewing your mind with *something.* Whatever that something is will shape your thought processes and decision-making. It will affect how you feel and what you think about the world. It will help you form opinions and worldviews. If something as seemingly innocuous as country music can shape a seventeen-year-old girl's heart with discontent, what is the constant scrolling of Instagram or the nightly bingeing of television programs doing to our hearts today? Scripture memorization helps us replace those worldly influences with solid truth that will shape our thought patterns in the best way possible.

The command in Romans 12 is not to conform to our old patterns of thinking but to be *transformed* by God's Word instead.

That's the promise! When we meditate on Scripture, the Holy Spirit uses Scripture to recontour our hearts and rewire our thinking. As a result, sanctified actions flow from a renewed mind and a transformed heart. This is an ongoing process that God is pleased to continue throughout our sanctification.[2] When our minds are renewed by Scripture, then we'll know how to live as His people. We'll see the differences in the ways of the world and the ways of Christ. We'll be able to discern what is wise and unwise, making decisions for God's glory rather than temporary satisfaction. We will be thinking like Him, not like the old us. But in order to do that, we must think about, meditate on, memorize His words.

Scripture-infused thinking will lead to Christ-centered living. Give God your mind and watch Him change your life.

MIND RENEWAL HELPS US STAY AWAKE

One of the more surprising effects of Scripture memorization on my life has been a growing discomfort with my entertainment choices. I've become acutely aware of both the quality *and* the quantity of the content I consume via shows and social media scrolling. What used to entertain me has more recently embarrassed me. What used to fill in gaps of time now tires me. Scrolling social media feels more like a numbing agent than a source of joy. Watching two hours of television before bed has felt like a burden more than a pleasure, and sometimes I wonder what it is I'm trying

---

2. I'm indebted to John Stott's helpful explanation of mind renewal in his commentary *The Message of Romans* (Downers Grove, IL: InterVarsity Press, 1994), 324.

to tamp down with my entertainment and leisure choices.

Please don't hear what I'm not saying. I'm not condemning television or social media altogether. I have a television and I watch it. I have streaming services and I use them. I have social media accounts and I access them regularly. What I *am* saying is that perpetual input from the world can have a stupefying and numbing effect on your mind and heart. Not only will the constant stream of cultural commentary desensitize you to immoral content, but it will divert you from the wholehearted worship we're called to in Romans 12. To put it bluntly, filling your mind with the noise of the world will put you to sleep spiritually, numbing you to the urgency and joy of wholehearted worship of Christ. John Piper writes:

> In this world of sleepwalking, the message is coming at you all day long—every day from television and from advertising and from all other kinds of things—to say, "Go to sleep, go to sleep, go to sleep with regard to God, with regard to Christ, with regard to the Bible." And the less you want the Bible, the less you want Jesus, the less you want God, the more effective you know the sleeping pills of the world have been in your life. And what [Paul's] saying here now is that faith and hope and love are the antidotes to the soporific effects of the world always trying to get you to go to sleep. So, combat that sleep-producing effect of the world by putting on faith and putting on hope and putting on love.[3]

———

3. John Piper, "Fighting for Faith in the Entertainment Age," Desiring God, July 20, 2022, https://www.desiringgod.org/interviews/fighting-for-faith-in-the-entertainment-age.

Whether we realize it or not, our entertainment habits have the potential to inoculate our hearts against wholehearted worship. So, it stands to reason that the way we fight "the soporific effects of the world" is by putting off our old ways of thinking and, instead, living and putting on Christ. How do we "put on Christ"? Paul explains: "Set your minds on things that are above, not on things that are on earth. For you have died, and your life is hidden with Christ in God" (Col. 3:2–3). We are to walk in holiness (rather than worldliness) because, Paul continues, we "have put off the old self with its practices and have put on the new self, which is being renewed in knowledge after the image of its creator" (Col. 3:9–10). Meditate on these verses with me for a moment, for they answer important questions that the enemy would like us to ignore or sleep through. *Who are you?* You are a new creation who has died to (given up, let go of, turned from) the old way of life as a slave to sin. *How are you supposed to live?* Be who you are in Christ, not who you used to be. Put to death the ongoing sin in your life by setting your mind on the things of God.

> **Fight spiritual sleepwalking with the Word.**

Don't miss that important phrase about the new self in verse 10: "the new self, which is being renewed in knowledge after the image of its creator." Your new self is being renewed as you grow in knowledge of God. This is ongoing—for the rest of your life. Don't let your old sinful habits and practices or constant, worldly pleasure-seeking lull you to sleep. Fight spiritual sleepwalking with the Word. Numbing yourself with the regular pursuit of mind-deadening experiences won't help you stay awake and live wholeheartedly for Christ. But regular meditation on Scripture will. The more you give your mind to the Word, the more easily you will walk away from the fleeting, soul-numbing pleasures of this world.

ATTRACTED BY REAL TREASURE

When you get into the habit of meditating on God's Word, you will, in time, notice the awakening of godly desires. You'll also observe things that used to hold attraction lose some of their shine. While Scripture meditation deepens your love for God, it also dilutes your love for the things of this world. The shows, music, books, and leisure pursuits that used to hold your attention won't satisfy like they once did. You'll feel conviction where you didn't in the past. Remember, the Bible isn't like any other book. It is God's inspired and inerrant Word. And with it, He can change the way you think and reshape your affections. Eventually, with a mind continually set on God's Word, you'll feel yourself at odds with this world, and that's a good thing. This isn't your home.

> When the world loses its hollow appeal because we know where our real treasure lies, then we will be well equipped to live in this world without being "of" it.

The author of Hebrews tells us that those who live by faith in Christ are citizens of a better country—a heavenly one whose builder and architect is God Himself (see Heb. 11:10–16). If our true home is with Him forever, then we shouldn't feel so at home in this life. The longer I walk with Jesus and meditate on His words, the more my heart yearns for my true home with Him in heaven.

It makes sense to me now when I feel out of step with my culture. I don't fret when I think about the brevity of life. I don't fear so much what people may do to me for holding to a worldview that clashes with theirs. This is not my home. I can rejoice when my heart finds more satisfaction in the glory of Christ than in the fleeting pleasures of earth. That's not to say that I don't enjoy my life here or ignore the blessings of family, good food, trips to the beach, friendships, or productive work. Those gifts of grace point me to the loveliness of a future untarnished by sin and sorrow and goodbyes. When the world loses its hollow appeal because we know where our real treasure lies, then we will be well equipped to live in this world without being "of" it. We will learn to make decisions with wisdom and discernment from a place of safety—of being hidden in God—rather than fear or pride.

If you have been memorizing Scripture and notice that your footing in this world feels different, rejoice in that. It's okay for the allures of earth to lose their shine, friend. The Lord is changing the way you think. You're thinking like Him. He is renewing your mind.

RENEWING YOUR MIND TAKES TIME

Remember when you joked in high school about studying for your history test via osmosis, holding your textbook to your forehead, and wishing you could bypass the studying process and just absorb it instead? (Or was that just me?) I can't really think of anything in this life that works like that. Change and growth take time.[4] When a believer in Jesus sets her heart and mind on His Word, the love for worldly living *will* fade in her life. Her desire to live for herself *will* dim. Her pattern of thinking *will* look more like the Lord's. She *will* become a wholehearted, living sacrifice.

But none of this will happen overnight. It takes time to renew your mind, to change and be changed. However, this is the gift of Scripture memorization. The sanctified changes in your thought life, the God-honoring way you make decisions, and the way you seek to live your whole life as spiritual worship unto the Lord grow from a lifetime of little moments of thinking deeply about His Word. Rolling those phrases around in your mouth over and over might seem rote at first, but with time, you will be changed by the good, strong words of the Lord.

Years from now, you'll exhibit growth and newness that you can't imagine today. Desires that dominated your thought life will be noticeably dimmer because, through daily meditation on His Word, God has shaped your mind and heart to look like His. On a regular day of mundane living, this might mean you work on memorization when you would ordinarily watch television or scroll your phone. What about those moments when you're commuting to work? Sitting in a carpool line? Folding a laundry mountain? Weeding the flower bed? Rocking a baby? Taking a walk? Grab hold of those moments when your mind is free to wander. Fill it with what is good and true so that with time, what is

---

4. I've written a book on the lifelong, ordinary work of sanctification in our lives. Check out *Everyday Faithfulness: The Beauty of Ordinary Perseverance in a Demanding World* for more on this subject.

good and true will flow from your mouth.

This might make Scripture memorization seem like a pile of little pieces of meditation throughout the day. That's exactly what it may be. But the pile adds up over time and becomes a treasure. The little moments when you recite "Do not be conformed to this world, but be transformed by the renewal of your mind" will eventu-

> As you mumble and recite and repeat and recount, the Lord is changing the way you think. And He is reminding you that you are His.

ally result in a renewed mind that is able to discern and obey. You might not think that much is happening in your slow, plodding commitment to Scripture memorization. I'll tell you what is happening as you mumble and recite and repeat and recount: the Lord is changing the way you think. He is changing your desires. He is keeping you awake to the spiritual battle going on for your affections and attention. He is reminding you that you are His. You will know how to go out and live wholeheartedly in a dark, confusing, world with the light and life of Christ because He is making you new. Word by word. Phrase by phrase. Day by day.

memorization tip

When it comes to passages that contain lists, like that of Colossians 3:12–14, consider the first letter of each item in the list. Can you form a sentence with those letters that will help you keep the words in proper order? In Colossians 3, Paul tells us to put on: compassionate hearts, kindness, humility, meekness, and patience. This is the time for a mnemonic device to help keep the correct order! What can you do with the letters C, K, H, M, and P that will make sense to *you*? I once used the names of several of my neighbors in a specific order because their names happened to work with a list in a passage I was memorizing. You can be creative with this—it only has to make sense to you!

suggested verses to memorize

Short form: Proverbs 4:23, Isaiah 29:13–18, Matthew 12:33–37,
        Romans 12:1–2, Ephesians 4:20–24,
        Colossians 3:1–4, 12–14
Long form: Isaiah 29, Matthew 12, Romans 12, Ephesians 4,
        Colossians 3

chapter 8

To Encourage
and Exhort

*And take not the word of truth utterly out of my mouth,
for my hope is in your rules.*

PSALM 119:43

y husband and I have an ongoing disagreement about the use of salt. He claims that salt makes food taste salty while I, the resident cook and in-house foodie, believe that salt brings out a food's natural flavor. The thing is, we're both right. Salt does enhance the food, brightening the notes of flavor. Even some desserts need salt to counterbalance the sweetness. But too much salt in any dish can ruin it. The trick lies in *how* you use salt. Knowing how to season food wisely can make or break a meal.

In Colossians 4, Paul encourages the church to walk in wisdom toward outsiders and to "let your speech always be gracious, seasoned with salt, so that you may know how you ought to answer each person" (Col. 4:6). Keeping the proper use of salt in mind, Paul's exhortation here is to use our speech in such a way that is full of grace, enhancing the gospel of Christ, when we speak to people outside the faith. Further, well-seasoned speech provides an answer to each person we come into contact with. Scripture gives us the words we need when encouraging our family of faith and when seeking to evangelize the lost. Storing God's words in our heart can aid us in speaking the right kind of encouragement to those who need it and sharing the gospel in a way that glorifies Jesus.

I don't know about you, but when it comes to knowing how to encourage others, I'm often guilty of improper seasoning. I either skip the salt altogether, offering weak platitudes that don't mean anything in the face of deep suffering, or I unload *every* truth and Scripture I can think of in a way that beats people down instead of building them up in Christ. Rather than oversalting with a heavy hand, we can use our words in such a way that adorns the gospel, making it appear lovely to those around us. We don't have to be afraid of well-seasoned speech. The Lord has given us what we need, and memorization can help us call to mind the words that season our speech with grace.

ENCOURAGEMENT GONE WRONG

The best way to *discourage* someone when you mean to build them up is to drop an unfiltered, generic platitude in their lap. We mean well, don't we? We want to encourage but we don't know what to say, so we stumble our way through one of those overused and misapplied Christian clichés. I used them plenty before I had ever known real suffering. But once you've walked through a significant trial or season of loss, you learn that paltry phrases loosely based on Scripture or firmly rooted in self offer no real or lasting encouragement.

The trouble with some of our favorite platitudes is that we serve them up with a can-do attitude and an encouragement for sufferers to "buck up." In so doing, we might unintentionally admonish sufferers for grieving their pain or losses at all. We learned that the Bible makes room for lament. Scripture gives space for grief, but some of our go-to sources of encouragement don't.

Some platitudes lack compassion, some lack truth, and some lack both. We might not realize we're offering "encouragement" without a particle of truth to them. Have you ever used any of these? Consider the biblical truth that counters these statements.

"God won't put on you more than you can handle!" Paul said, "All who desire to live a godly life in Christ Jesus will be persecuted" (2 Tim. 3:12).

"God wants you to be happy!" Paul said, "For this is the will of God, your sanctification" (1 Thess. 4:3).

"When God closes a door, He opens a window!" The author of Hebrews said, "Be content with what you have, for [God] has said, 'I will never leave you nor forsake you'" (Heb. 13:5).

In her book on encouragement, Lindsey Carlson writes: "We need encouragement that rightly assures us that we do not have all we need on our own and that we cannot help ourselves; we need to 'know the love of Christ that surpasses knowledge' in order to be filled with the fullness of God (Eph. 3:19)."[1] The platitudes we offer when we're not sure what to say might sound right or apt in the moment, but in the end they don't offer true hope or encouragement.

What our brothers and sisters in Christ need are truer, deeper words that point them not to hope in changed circumstances or personal resolve to survive but to *Christ* upon whom their every breath depends. We need to give them the truth and hope that is found in Jesus' victory over sin, Satan, and death at the cross and the empty tomb. And we need to offer it with the compassion with which the Lord saw and loved those who were lost and hurting (see Matt. 9:36). If God did not spare sending His own Son to save us, won't He always give us what we truly need to persevere in faithfulness? God didn't just save us and then leave us to our own devices. No, He sanctifies us every day, molding our hearts and shaping us to be like Christ. He is not immune to our hurts, trials, or challenges. He hears our prayers and welcomes our worries into His capable hands. These are the truths the discouraged heart needs to hear, and they come straight from Scripture.[2] Yes, "God's got this," but we need to know why and how and when and through whom.

----

1. Lindsey Carlson, *A Better Encouragement: Trading Self-Help for True Hope* (Wheaton, IL: Crossway Books, 2022), 55.
2. Romans 8:31–32; 7:29; Hebrews 4:15–16.

RIGHT ENCOURAGEMENT USED WRONG

What might be worse than some of our favorite Christian*ish* cheers is the *manner* in which we offer them. When you use salt wisely in cooking, the diner leaves the meal with a memorable experience of expertly flavored cuisine. Too much salt, however, obliterates the taste of food. The salty experience is all that is remembered—the misuse of seasoning, not the flavor of the food itself. Similarly, we can use God's Word in the wrong way. While we mean well, our mishandling of Scripture when trying to encourage can leave the other person with a bad taste in their mouth. There are two kinds of encouragers I've seen mishandle God's Word, and unfortunately, I've been both of them at one time or another.

The (Well-Meaning) Hammer

I remember hearing a podcaster talk once about being a tool the Lord could use to reach other people with the gospel. Her pastor had gently admonished her one day with "There are lots of tools to use for the kingdom. You don't always have to be a hammer!"[3] Have you ever used Scripture to theoretically beat people over the head with truth? I have! Sometimes our passion for truth can undermine our attempt to encourage. It is absolutely true that God works all things together for the good of those who love Him and are called according to His purpose (see Rom. 8:28), but brightly reciting that

---

3. I wish I could remember where I heard this conversation, but it's been many years and I cannot recall what podcast or speaker used this illustration. I'm thankful for their wisdom, though, for I refer to it often.

truth when a friend is sifting through the remains of a shattered life might not be the most sensitive way to encourage them with God's Word. The Lord tells us in Proverbs that "whoever sings songs to a heavy heart is like one who takes off a garment on a cold day" (Prov. 25:20).

Insensitivity can ruin our attempts to encourage. It takes presence in relationship and persistence in Scripture meditation to rightly use God's Word to comfort someone who is suffering. Are you sitting with your friend in their suffering or just spitting out Scriptures about a good ending? Don't quote Scripture if you're unwilling to enter the suffering of others. Remind your friend of God's love and care in Scripture while keeping watch with them through their dark night of the soul. You can apply His Word as a balm instead of a hammer.

> The manner in which we deliver God's Word to a troubled heart matters.

If your desire to encourage someone is divorced from your prayers for them, take time to first pray over the Scriptures you want them to hear and know. Do you want your friend to know that God will work good from her current circumstances? Romans 8:28 might be the Scripture you've memorized for the express purpose of encouragement—and that's a good thing!—but pull back a little farther and check the context. Read the preceding verses, memorize them, pray them.

But if we hope for what we do not see, we wait for it with patience. Likewise the Spirit helps us in our weakness. For we do not know what to pray for as we ought, but the Spirit himself intercedes for us with groanings too deep for words. And he who searches hearts knows what is the mind of the Spirit, because the Spirit intercedes for the saints according to the will of God. And we know that for those who love God all things work together for good, for those who are called according to his purpose. For those whom he foreknew he also predestined to be conformed to the image of his Son, in order that he might be the firstborn among many brothers. And those whom he predestined he also called, and those whom he called he also justified, and those whom he justified he also glorified. (Rom. 8:25–30)

Meditate on these verses with your friend in mind. Pray Romans 8:25–30 for her, knowing the Spirit will intercede in ways you cannot. Write your friend a note telling her you're praying for God to keep His promise to never waste her suffering, to draw near to her in trials, and to know that the Holy Spirit is praying for her because He loves her. We can trust God to work our sufferings for good because He has ordained our salvation, sanctification, and glorification. He has written a good story, even if the current chapter is hard.

The manner in which we deliver God's Word to a troubled heart matters. Season your speech with God's Word but do so with care. Your discouraged friend doesn't need you to shout Romans 8:28 in her face when she is in the valley of the shadow of death. She needs you to pray it with confidence when you're in her living room, holding her hand, sitting with her in her suffering.

The (Unintentional) Heretic

Sometimes we encourage with biblical truth (that's good!) but not in proper context (that's bad!). I cannot tell you how many times people tried to encourage me with verses about Sarah and Hannah and Elizabeth during my first decade of infertility. Being pretty unfamiliar with the Bible during those years, I grabbed hold of those "promises" as if they were mine, hoping against hope that God's promise to Hannah in the temple was mine to claim. Imagine my disappointment with the Lord, then, when *I never once conceived*. Was God a liar? Or were those verses not meant to be used in the way I had used them? Sarah, Hannah, and Elizabeth had specific promises from God that they would give birth to specific children who would play specific parts in the redemption story of the Bible. Those weren't my promises to claim. Twisting verses out of context set me up to loathe Him when He failed to deliver what He had, in fact, never promised me.

I don't blame the well-meaning encouragers; I should have studied the Word more closely to understand context and promises. But I've learned from those situations that encouraging others with Scriptures I've not meditated on can be problematic. We rarely intend to be heretics, but without spending time digging into Scripture and thinking deeply on God's words, we might inadvertently share heretical encouragement that won't serve others well. God doesn't always give us what we want, even if we see our desires satisfied in the lives of people in the Bible. But we do know that Jesus won't break a bruised reed, that His yoke is gentle and provides true rest (see Isa. 42:3; Matt. 11:28–30). So while we can and should encourage those who are grieving losses or living with deferred hopes with Scripture, we must be certain that we are handling God's Word properly. There are promises that are generally true for every believer, but there are also promises that were meant for certain people at a certain time in redemptive history.

Jen Wilkin helps us understand the difference between principle and promise:

> Promises are always fulfilled 100% of the time. Principles state general truths. The book of Proverbs is often mistaken for a book of promises, when in fact it is a book of principles. The principle of "train up a child in the way he should go and when he is old he will not depart from it" is generally true and is wise to heed. But it is not a guarantee that every child who is raised with godly instruction will become a believer.[4]

She goes on to say that we often misunderstand how promises are kept in Scripture when we ignore the original context.

> We often apply a promise to ourselves before considering its original audience or its historical, cultural or textual context. In some cases, a promise was made to a specific person for a specific reason and has no further application beyond its immediate context. In other cases, the application can only be properly made after the promise is understood in its original

---

4. Jen Wilkin, "Which Promises Are for Me?," Jen Wilkin (blog), November 13, 2014, https://www.jenwilkin.net/blog/2014/11/which-promises-are-for-me.html.

context. God's promise to Abram of land and offspring cannot be taken to mean God will give me a house or children. It can, however, be applied to mean he will give me a spiritual inheritance through Christ.[5]

When we use God's Word to encourage others, we must pay attention to the broader context so that we don't offer promises that God never made. Memorization provides us the opportunity to first think deeply about the verses we want to share with those who are discouraged and hurting. When we commit to learning longer chunks of Scripture—whole chapters or entire books—we can avoid making promises God did not make. Again, most of us don't mean to be heretics, but poor study and understanding of God's Word can lead us down a heretical path. No matter how well-intentioned we are, our biblical encouragement will carry far more weight when it is rooted in truth and proper context.

If your sister in Christ is fighting a difficult battle in her personal life, go to promises that are true for all believers, reminding her of her future inheritance with Christ when all suffering will one day cease. "And after you have suffered a little while, the God of all grace, who has called you to his eternal glory in Christ, will himself restore, confirm, strengthen, and establish you" (1 Peter 5:10). God has equipped us well for the Christian life. He has given us a treasure of truths to encourage and build up our brothers and sisters in Christ. The apostle Paul encouraged the early church

---

5. Jen Wilkin, "Which Promises Are for Me?"

numerous times to build one another up in the Lord. What better way to do that than with the Lord's own words?

As you meditate on the words of God, pray and share them with wisdom. Ask the Spirit to help you comfort others with the words that have comforted you. Let the weeks and months that you spend memorizing a passage help you understand its greater context so that when you share it, it truly applies. And look at the hurting with compassion like our Savior did. Let truth be graciously offered with the kindest, wisest seasoning.

SCRIPTURE MEMORIZATION FOR EVANGELISM

Regular meditation on Scripture will change the way we speak to others. Donald Whitney wrote that "true success is promised to those who meditate on God's Word, who think deeply on Scripture, not just at one time each day, but at moments throughout the day and night. They meditate so much that Scripture saturates their conversation. The fruit of their meditation is action."[6] The success he refers to is walking in obedience that is blessed by the Lord. We're not talking about material blessing here. We're talking about spiritual growth and fruitfulness. What we pour into our hearts will come out, and it will shape both us and those around us. Even those who don't know Christ.

Jesus commissioned His disciples, and all who have followed Him, to "go therefore and make disciples of all nations, baptizing

---

6. Donald S. Whitney, *Spiritual Disciplines for the Christian Life* (Colorado Springs, CO: NavPress, 1991), 48.

them in the name of the Father and of the Son and of the Holy Spirit, teaching them to observe all that I have commanded you" (Matt. 28:19–20). It is our duty and our privilege to share the name of Christ with a lost and dying world. We who have tasted and seen that the Lord is good are tasked with sharing the beautiful, good news of salvation for all who believe in Christ for the atonement of sins. It is indeed an honor to be included in the building of God's kingdom. But if I'm honest, sharing the gospel with an unbeliever can sometimes be the scariest conversation imaginable because I simply don't know what to say. If you have felt this way before, the good news is you're not alone. The better news is that Jesus promised to help us in situations exactly like this.

> We might find ourselves fearful of freezing in silence or blurting out the wrong words. But Jesus has promised that in these crucial moments our words about *who He is* matter the most.

Whenever I'm in conversations with unbelievers, I find myself praying for the Spirit to give me an open door to share truth with them. Paul models this in Colossians 4, asking the church to pray for God to open a door for the Word so that he can declare the mystery of Christ clearly, which is how he "ought to speak" (see Col. 4:2–4). Clear, gospel-infused words are what we need when speaking to unbelievers. And the Lord will provide what we need when we need it.

Consider these words of Christ to His disciples about future persecution as His followers: "When they deliver you over, do not be anxious how you are to speak or what you are to say, for what you are to say will be given to you in that hour. For it is not you who speak, but the Spirit of your Father speaking through you" (Matt. 10:19–20). While our everyday gospel conversations with those who aren't Christians might not look like inquisitions before hostile authoritarians, we might still find ourselves fearful of freezing in silence or blurting out the wrong words. But Jesus has promised that in these crucial moments when our words about who He is matter the most, the Spirit will speak through us. And if the word of Christ is dwelling in us richly, as Paul exhorted in Colossians 3, then His words will flow through us to those who need to hear them.

We must depend on the Spirit to supply what we need when looking for ways to thread the gospel into our conversations, yet we can also do the preemptive work of hiding Scripture in our hearts so that we have a well of truth to draw from. You might consider memorizing key verses so that you can quickly walk through the truth about God, man, sin, and the work of Christ at the cross.[7]

But you don't have to be that specific. Regular meditation on large passages of Scripture will come up in many different ways to share Christ with an unbelieving neighbor or coworker. Again, the more you think about Scripture, the more it will come out in your conversations. Memorizing a passage that doesn't even *seem* to be about evangelism or salvation can be a catalyst for sharing Christ in a gospel conversation. Even a discussion about why or what you're memorizing can turn your discussion to Christ.

---

7. For example, Romans 3:23; 6:23; 5:8; 10:9–10; 10:13.

We don't memorize Scripture to keep it to ourselves. Though many of the benefits will be ours, internalizing God's Word will undoubtedly serve those around you. As you flood your mind and heart with biblical truth, the overflow will saturate your conversations, prayers, and desires. What a beautiful thing to be a mouthpiece for the good words of the Lord! Let your words be salty and flavorful, infused with the true, encouraging Word of God.

---

memorization tip

Make a plan to memorize passages specifically for encouragement and evangelism so that you have a reservoir of Scriptures to draw from when you find yourself in conversation with someone who is discouraged or who needs the hope of the gospel. Additionally, consider the passages you have *already* memorized. How might they be applied to a friend who is struggling? How could they be used to plant gospel seeds in a conversation with an unbeliever?

suggested verses to memorize

Short form: Psalm 34:18, Matthew 10:19–20, Romans 3:23, 6:23, 5:8, 10:9–10, 10:13, Romans 8:28, 1 Peter 5:10
Long form: Psalm 34, Psalm 62, Ephesians 2:1–10, 3:14–21, 1 Peter

---

---

chapter 9

For All of Life

I have chosen the way of faithfulness;
I set your rules before me.

PSALM 119:30

*L*ast Christmas, I sat next to my ninety-five-year-old grand-mother at my parents' breakfast table and chatted long after the dishes were washed and put away. My grandmother, whom we call "Ma," has long treasured God's Word, and she can quote long portions of it from years of studying, teaching, and meditating on it.

Several years ago, she lost much of her vision after suffering a retinal bleed, so it's been long time since she's had the ability to pick up a book and read. While she loves a good inspirational memoir, the greatest loss by far was her ability to read her Bible whenever she wanted. At the table that morning, while we talked about the Bible (her favorite subject), she rattled off a constellation of Scriptures to me. They didn't all come from the same part of the Bible, but they were connected by a thread of supplication. I asked her to repeat it, and she did—verbatim. She explained that the Lord had brought these different verses to mind, and she'd woven them into a prayer she prays every morning and evening. Buried deep in the crevices and folds of her well-used mind, the words of Scripture reverberate and continue to infuse her thinking, praying, and living. Maybe more now than ever.

Pay attention to this, I thought while she talked. *This is the kind of life you want.* And many months removed from that breakfast table encouragement, that's still the kind of life I want. No matter how many years the Lord gives me in this life, I want to sit across a table from a younger believer, encouraging her with Scriptures that have been etched on my heart for decades. I want a life that is shaped by the Word of God.

Since you've made it to the last chapter of a book on Scripture memorization, you probably desire a life like my grandmother's too. (I'll share her with you. Everybody needs a Ma in their life. She would absolutely *love* you.) We want to get to the end of our lives and speak with wise, well-seasoned speech. We want to feel secure in God's love for us. We want to stand firm on the truth of the gospel through many light and momentary trials. And we want to see that future glory that awaits us because we are *so convinced* that God's Word is true and lasting and bursting with promises that will prove true when we close our eyes to this life and open them to our realest life to come.

We won't acquire a Scripture-shaped life without the ongoing, transformative work that God does over time with His Word. If we want to employ the gifts of wisdom and discernment, if we want to stand firmly on truth, if we want to be certain of God's love and care for us in every circumstance, then we must flood our minds with the living and active Word of God.

We learn from the apostle Paul that the sacred writings of Scripture are able to make us "wise for salvation" (2 Tim. 3:15), so we need the truth of them to come to faith in Jesus in the first place. But we still need the Word for its sanctifying effect on all parts of our life in Christ afterward, as we've discussed throughout this book. Paul explains that "all Scripture is breathed out by God and profitable for teaching, for reproof, for correction, and for training in righteousness, that the man of God may be complete, equipped for every good work" (2 Tim. 3:16–17). We will never outgrow our need for God's Word nor its shaping, renewing, refining effect on our thoughts and actions. Burying it deep in our minds and hearts now will serve us later in life in ways we could never imagine. God sanctifies in so many ways; it isn't possible in one book to fully plumb the depths of the benefits and blessings of hiding His words in your heart.

> The more you allow His words to run the neural pathways of your brain, the more you pile up treasures of Scripture in your heart.

But as I've learned, observed others, and applied the practice of memorization and meditation to my own life, I can attest to the sweet, purifying work that God is pleased to do in a heart that lives and breathes His Word. The more you allow His words to run the neural pathways of your brain, the more you pile up treasures of Scripture in your heart—the more your life will look like one that is lived in and from the Word. There will be less of you and more of Him. And that, in the end, is what every person who walks with Jesus needs the most. More, more, *more* of Him. Because whether we realize it or not, our hearts will always want Him the most. We were created *for* Him (see Col. 1:16; Rev. 4:11).

FOR GETTING WISDOM

When I think of a Scripture-shaped life, I automatically think of wisdom. I have this vision of myself later in life where I, gray-haired and wrinkled, graciously dole out heaps of lived wisdom to younger women. I'm doing really well on the gray hair and wrinkles part of that vision, but not so much on the lived wisdom. I feel achingly short on wisdom.

During the summer that I wrote the majority of this book, one of my children received some difficult medical news. As we've spent countless hours driving to and from the children's hospital for appointments in another city, rearranged our lives around surgery, and tried to parent our child through a very difficult new normal, I've felt desperate for wisdom. *Am I making the right decisions? Why was there no user's manual for parenting through this kind of thing? Did I say the right thing to encourage my son? Am I showing him how to hold on to Jesus or am I teaching him to become bitter?* I've combed my Bible for help, reading the book of Proverbs multiple times with a highlighter and a box of tissues. To be sure, the book of wisdom did not fall short. I learned through it that wisdom comes from God, from seeking Him, from walking closely with Him, from staying far from the entanglements of sin. But mostly, the words of Proverbs quietly reminded me time and again of the passage I memorized three years ago from the book of James:

> If any of you lacks wisdom, let him ask God, who gives gener-
> ously to all without reproach, and it will be given him. But let
> him ask in faith, with no doubting, for the one who doubts
> is like a wave of the sea that is driven and tossed by the wind.
> For that person must not suppose that he will receive any-
> thing from the Lord; he is a double-minded man, unstable in
> all his ways. (James 1:5–8)

Three whole years before my daily, desperate pleas for wisdom, the Lord had already planted the answer in my heart through memorization. It dawned on me early one morning while pray-ing and worrying (but mostly worrying): I *already* know how to get wisdom. It comes from God who showers it generously on all who ask. The one caveat is that we simply walk in the wisdom He gives us, rather than questioning and overanalyzing it. So I prayed. And I realized that the Lord had already given me the wisdom I needed because He was shaping my heart through Scripture memorization. When I was tempted to question the steps in front of me, I remembered those words I'd rehearsed and recited in my shower and on my morning walks for weeks on end: "for the one who doubts is like a wave of the sea that is driven and tossed by the wind." I didn't want to be hurled from tempest to tempest. I wanted to stand firm on the truth that God has given

> "You're different,"
> she said. "A few years
> ago, this would have
> sent you over the edge
> of anxiety and worry."

me what I need to persevere in this life, in this very season.

A friend from church checked in on me recently to see how things were going after an important doctor's appointment for our son. I explained the next steps we were facing. I told her I felt peace that I knew was from the Lord, and that I hadn't expected it to be like this. "You're different," she said. "A few years ago, this would have sent you over the edge of anxiety and worry." I laughed because I feel like I *live* on the edge of anxiety and worry much of the time. But I knew what she meant. I was different—not because I'm strong or resilient or full of stamina. I assure you, I am none of those things (just ask my friend). I'm different because the Lord has changed me, renewing my mind and deepening my trust in Him through His Word. The words of James that were buried in my heart years ago blossomed with comfort and certainty when I needed them most. That is encouragement enough for me to continue hiding Scripture in my heart for the rest of my life.

If wisdom is something you long for like I do, if you have a picture of your future self exuding peace and living with discernment, begin memorizing Scripture *today*. You could make a list of the Scriptures that speak of wisdom and discernment and commit them to memory (James 1:5–8; 3:13–18; 1 Cor. 3:18; anything from Proverbs). But you could also pick *any* passage, *any* chapter, *any* book of the Bible—hide it in your heart, and watch the Lord shape your thought processes and reactions to look more like His.

You don't have to limit yourself to topical memorization because *all* of Scripture is useful for teaching and training in righteousness. Every last word.

FOR CERTAIN LOVE

One of the more surprising blessings of Scripture memorization I've enjoyed is a deeper confidence in God's love for me. My upbringing in the church is something I am deeply thankful for. I love the local church and will never live my life outside the safety and encouragement of the family of God. But as fallible creatures we don't always get it right. An erroneous form of teaching crept into the culture of my childhood church, praising a certain type of "good" behavior—dressing in a specific way, educating your children in a specific way, and avoiding specific vices—to the extent that those who met this "good" standard seemed much more loved by God than those who lived with a bit more Christian freedom. Though neither my parents nor my pastor taught this behavior-driven brand of Christianity, I still noticed the way people lived it out in our community of faith and judged myself accordingly. As a result, I struggled for *decades* connecting the dots between obedience to God and being loved by God. If I didn't meet the right standard, would He love me less? If I obeyed better than someone else, did He love me more?

Deep study of God's Word over the last ten years of my life has untangled a good deal of my former misunderstandings about grace and "good" behavior. But it was Scripture memorization that dealt the final blow to my faulty belief that God didn't love me as much as He loved His other children. The passages that flipped the switch for me weren't even about love, specifically. Or obedience. They were verses, even paragraphs about Him. Lists of the Lord's character qualities, doxologies about His divinity and everlasting nature. A few I've mentioned already in this book, but here are some verses from the passages I have memorized over the years that showed me just how God loves His people.

> God's love was never based on my obedience or goodness in the first place. It was based on *His* goodness.

Oh, the depths of the riches and wisdom and knowledge of God! How unsearchable are his judgments and how inscrutable his ways! For who has known the mind of the Lord, or who has been his counselor? Or who has given a gift to him that he might be repaid? For from him and through him and to him are all things. To him be the glory forever. Amen. (Rom. 11:33–36)

Who shall bring any charge against God's elect? It is God who justifies. Who is to condemn? Christ Jesus is the one who died—more than that, who was raised—who is at the right hand of God, who indeed is interceding for us. Who shall separate us from the love of Christ? (Rom. 8:33–35)

He is the image of the invisible God, the firstborn of all creation. For by him all things were created, in heaven and on earth, visible and invisible, whether thrones or dominions or rulers or authorities—all things were created through him and for him. And he is before all things and in him all things hold together. And he is the head of the body, the church. He is the beginning, the firstborn from the dead, that in everything he might be preeminent. For in him all the fullness of God was pleased to dwell and through him to reconcile to himself all things, whether on earth or in heaven, making peace by the blood of his cross. (Col. 1:15–20)

God is our refuge and strength, a very present help in trouble. Therefore we will not fear though the earth gives way, though the mountains be moved into the heart of the sea, though its waters roar and foam, though the mountains tremble at its swelling. . . . The LORD of hosts is with us; the God of Jacob is our fortress. (Ps. 46:1–3, 7)

The more I rehearsed, recited, and remembered the truth about God's holiness, His goodness, His unfathomable grace in stooping low to bring sinful people into His family through faith in Jesus, the more certain I became of His immovable, unbreakable love for me. God's love was never based on my obedience or goodness in the first place. It was based on *His* goodness.

But I'm not sure I would have grasped that truth so clearly if I hadn't had to roll the words about His character around in my mouth and mind day in and day out. When I was cooking dinner: "through *him* to reconcile to himself all things." When I was lying awake at night with insomnia and anxiety: "God is our refuge and strength, a very present help in trouble." When I confessed my sin *again* to the Lord: "It is God who justifies." When I compared my obedience to someone else's: "Who is to condemn? Christ Jesus is the one who died."

> Scripture is no empty word. It is your very life.

139

The practice of Scripture memorization placed God's Word where I needed it when I needed it. The Holy Spirit continually brings verses and passages to mind when I'm struggling with sin or fear or pain. It's true that the Spirit can encourage and remind you of any truth in any way He pleases, but He will often use the very words you are committing to memory to encourage you. Scripture is no empty word. It is your very life. When it is in your mouth and before your eyes and in your heart, the Lord will use it to remind you of who He is, who you are, and how deeply and utterly loved you are (see Deut. 32:47; 30:14).

FOR LASTING HOPE

It would be easy to end this book with a promise that if you memorize Scripture, you'll be happy and joyful all the time. That may, in fact, be what you want from me at this point. But I can't guarantee that hiding God's Word in your heart will free you from trials or experiences that make you sad or draw you down the path of suffering. Actually, if you are in Christ, I can guarantee you the opposite. You *will* have trouble in this world. You *will* endure hard things. You *will* have to practice perseverance until you see Jesus face-to-face. Scripture memorization doesn't exempt you from those things. But it *will* carry you through them. God's Word was meant to lead us to salvation, aid us in our sanctification, equip us for godly living, and provide us with a lasting hope that carries us from this day until *the* day when Christ Jesus will return for us.

One of the things I love about memorizing Scripture is how slow the process is. It is *not* a quick path. Memorization takes a lot of time and regular work. But that is kind of the point. The plodding work of wrapping our minds around phrases, sentences, and lists forces us to slowly think through verses we might otherwise have skipped over. I might think I know what a passage says or means, but undoubtedly, when I begin to memorize it, I am presented with a much deeper understanding and comprehension of what God is actually saying. It's a pleasure every time.

I had that experience recently while meditating through some passages in Romans. Right in the middle of a section where Paul is giving instructions on living with one another in the church in an understanding, selfless way, he reminds us of the purpose of Scripture. I must have read this verse dozens of times in my life, but mumbling the words aloud forced me to slow down and really hear what Paul is saying: "For whatever was written in former days was written for our instruction, that through endurance and through the encouragement of the Scriptures we might have hope" (Rom. 15:4). *Hope!* This is why Scripture memorization is so vitally important to the Christian life. What was written down for us in Scripture—long before you or I existed—was given for our instruction, our endurance, our encouragement, and our hope. If God gave us His Word to carry us through life, why wouldn't we latch on to it with all our heart, soul, mind, and strength? It is useful for every part of the Christian life! And meditating on Scripture regularly will engender

> **Open your Bible, choose a chapter, print it out, place it where it will be ever before your eyes, and start mumbling and memorizing it today.**

deeper affection for the One who gave it to us in the first place.

We have hope, eternal hope that will far outlast this world, because God has saved us through faith in Jesus and has given us His Word to sustain us until we see Him. If I could exhort or encourage you in any way, it would be to open your Bible, choose a chapter, print it out, place it where it will be ever before your eyes, and start mumbling and memorizing it today.

When you need hope tomorrow or next year or twenty years from now, the truth of the verses you memorize today will well up in your heart with encouragement and certainty. While you recite at the kitchen sink or rehearse in the shower or mumble aloud on your commute to work, the Lord will shape your heart little by little, phrase by phrase. He'll renew your mind while you commit His words to memory.

Memorizing Scripture is never about a destination of recitation. It is all about the journey of treasuring God's Word in your heart. Pile it up. Store it in heaps. Let it change the way you think. Remember it. Remember it. *Remember it*. Scripture was written to give you hope.

memorization tip

If you've fallen out of the habit of memorization or gotten bogged down in a passage for a really long time, do not be discouraged! Don't quit altogether. Start again. Choose a new passage or go back to the beginning of an old one and refresh your habits. What worked in the last season of life might not work for this season. Maybe your learning style has changed to accommodate your life circumstances. If you've focused on writing the Word in the past, try listening to it instead. Ask a friend to memorize with you or invite your family into the process for accountability and new enthusiasm. Just don't quit. Remember this isn't a race. It's a journey of treasuring God's Word. You're not behind.

suggested verses to memorize

Short form: Deuteronomy 32:45–47, Psalm 46:1–3,
Proverbs 2:6–15, Romans 11:33–36, Romans 15:4,
2 Timothy 3:15–17
Long form: Deuteronomy 32, Psalm 46, Proverbs 2, Romans, 2
Timothy 3

There is therefore now no condemnation for those who are in Christ Jesus. For the law of the Spirit of life has set you free in Christ Jesus from the law of sin and death. For God has done what the law, weakened by the flesh, could not do. By sending his own Son in the likeness of sinful flesh and for sin, he condemned sin in the flesh, in order that the righteous requirement of the law might be fulfilled in us, who walk not according to the flesh but according to the Spirit. For those who live according to the flesh set their minds on the things of the flesh, but those who live according to the

Memorization Resources

his list of resources is intended both to help you memorize Scripture and inspire you to do so. Note that some resources are free, some require investment, and some are included to remind you that you *can* memorize and to give you the courage to do so.

JOURNALS AND VERSE CARDS

Journibles are lined journals designed for copying Scripture word for word. (https://www.heritagebooks.org/categories/journibles/)

Topical Memory System from The Navigators provides a workbook, pocket-sized printed cards, and a card holder designed to help you memorize Scriptures pertaining to topics like proclaiming Christ and growth in Christlikeness. (https://www.navigators.org/resource/topical-memory-system/)

Fighter Verses from Desiring God include fifty-two passages per year, for five years, to help you memorize Scripture. Weekly devotionals are included to help you meditate on each week's passage.[†] (https://www.fighterverses.com/about-us)

The Daily Grace Co. provides multiple sets of 4x4 inch verse cards. Some sets are grouped around themes like grief or seasons of waiting, and some sets are blank to allow you to handwrite your chosen verses and references. (https://thedailygraceco.com/)

APPS

Dwell Bible Audio Bible App comes with many customizable features that allow you to listen to Scripture in a way that suits your learning style. You can choose the Bible translation, the narrator, the background music or ambient sounds, and the speed at which the passage is read. You can also repeat passages as often as you want for memorization purposes or set a sleep timer for Scripture to be read to you until you fall asleep.[§]

The Voxer App is intended for communication with others but allows you to send audio notes to yourself. You can recite your passages while recording on Voxer and then play it back to rehearse or listen for errors. Or, you can record while reading your selected passage aloud and use it in place of an audio Bible.

The Verses App allows you to create a group of friends with whom you can set a memorization goal and practice together, noting one another's progress.[†§]

MUSIC

"Psalms, Hymns, and Spiritual Songs" album by Shane & Shane[§]

Seeds Family Worship albums*

"Jesus Kids" album by Shai Linne*

"Worship in the Word" albums by Shane & Shane and Kingdom Kids*

BOOKS

Read It, See It, Say It, Sing It: Knowing and Loving the Bible by Hunter Beless*

His Word in My Heart by Janet Pope

An Approach to Extended Memorization of Scripture by Andrew M. Davis (ebook)

A Call to Scripture Memory by Susan Heck

Spiritual Disciplines for the Christian Life by Donald S. Whitney

Praying the Bible by Donald S. Whitney

Remember: The Science of Memory and the Art of Forgetting by Lisa Genova

SUBSCRIPTION SERVICES

Dwell Differently uses the first letter method for their temporary tattoos. They design a tattoo around a verse of Scripture and work in the first letter of each word of text into the design. By applying their temporary tattoos to your wrist or hand, you can look at the design often, reciting the passage based on the first letters of each word. Their designs come in black and white, working with every skin tone. By the time the tattoo disappears, you've stored that verse in your heart. Bonus: when someone sees your tattoo, you have an excellent talking point for a gospel conversation! *† (https://dwelldifferently.com)

Bible Memory Project provides a monthly subscription that includes bookmarks, wristbands, stickers, and a 4x6 print with each themed verse. The wristbands use the first letter method.*† (https://biblememproject.com)

SIMPLE TOOLS/METHODS

The Verse Card Maker. Utilizing the VCM website will allow you to type and print your own verse cards so you can memorize at your own pace without having to handwrite anything. (http://www.mcscott.org/index.html)

Ziplock bags. Handwrite or type and print your chosen text. Slide the printed text upside down into a gallon-sized ziplock bag. Tape the bag, zipper side down, to the wall of your shower so you can work on memorization each time you take a shower.*§

Index cards. Write your text on index cards and set them in places you will see on a regular basis: dashboard of your vehicle, desk, kitchen windowsill, bathroom mirror.

Open Bible. Rather than closing your Bible when you're done with your devotion time, leave it open to your chosen passage and stop to read and recite each time you walk by your Bible.

Around-the-Table Game. If you are working on memorization with your family, use mealtimes to work on your verses. Have one person start with the first word of the text, and then let the next person take the next subsequent word, working in a circle until you reach the end of the passage. Next time, begin with a different person or go in the opposite direction to change up the order. Note: this game will usually result in lots of laughter.*†§

---

* Can be used with children
† Works well when memorizing with another individual or a group
§ Glenna's regular tools for memorization

Acknowledgments

*I*n the early stages of this book, an editor asked me, "Why are you the person to write a book on Scripture memorization?" It's a standard question for every book idea, but I paused, uncertain of how to answer. The truth is, I am nobody important. I'm just me. I'm not a professor. I don't have a seminary degree. I don't have any special credentials that qualify me for a task like this. I am a wife, mom, writer, and weekly Bible study leader for an extremely small group of women. But I will tell you what I told the editor: "I am the person to write this book because Scripture memorization has changed my life and I can't stop talking about it." Trust me, if you walk the path of Scripture memory, you will see what I mean. Once you taste and see that the Lord's Word is sweet to your mouth and life-giving to your heart, you won't stop talking about it. To that end, I want to thank all the people who have listened to me talk about Scripture memorization, have practiced it with me, and have believed that I was the person to write this book.

I am so grateful for my acquisitions editor, Catherine Parks, who not only helped me think through this project and offered helpful edits and suggestions but who also prayed me through from start to finish. I was blessed by her care for both my work and my soul. She believed in this book from day one, and I am so thankful. Many thanks to my developmental editor, Pam Pugh, for her careful edits and encouragement! I'm grateful to the entire team at Moody for getting behind a project like this because they believe that God's people will be blessed by memorizing God's Word. What a joy to work with you all! Special thanks to Leah and Nathan Finn for their God-directed suggestion of what to do with this book idea. I've so appreciated your support for this project, especially when I knocked over a can of sparkling water onto my laptop.

To the women of my Tuesday afternoon Bible study, you put up with a *lot* of talk about memorization. Thank you for listening, for helping me dig deep into the Word each week, and for letting me verbally process with you after too many hours of writing in solitude. To the people of Grace Bible Fellowship, thank you for regularly asking about my writing and praying for me on long writing days. I am beyond blessed to call you family.

For my mother and grandmothers who have shared their lived wisdom through their loved Bibles, I will never cease to be thankful. A heritage of faith in Jesus and commitment to His Word is a profound gift of grace.

To my sons, Isaiah and Ian, thank you for giving me the time to write, especially during that one summer when I had to tell all the neighbor kids to go home so I could get some work done. Your patience in having a writing mom is a kindness that I cherish.

Thank you for indulging me in my passion for memorization. Dinnertime is never boring with you two to purposefully butcher every passage we learn. I love you both so much.

To my husband, William, who believes in every project I take on, cheers me on when I am discouraged, and talks me through all the theological points when I'm stuck, I am blessed to be your wife. Most husbands want their wives to be happy. You want yours to *flourish*. I love you more than I can say. (And you know I have a *lot* of words.)

To Jesus, the Word made flesh—thank You for upholding me with Your strong, right hand while I wrote. May this book lead Your people to love You and hide Your unchanging, unfading Word in their hearts. Thank You for giving us everything we need to endure and to have hope. The grass withers and the flowers fall, but Your Word remains forever.

Don't just read the Bible literally—
read it *Literarily*.

A single approach doesn't do justice to the variety of genres that make up the Word of God. In *Literarily*, Kristie Anyabwile reveals the value of studying the Bible literarily—that is, according to the literary style presented in a particular book, chapter, or passage.

978-0-8024-2399-3 | also available as an eBook and audiobook

A joy-filled, thoughtful, and realistic pathway
through the entirety of God's Word!

Bible Studies for Women

IN-DEPTH. CHRIST-CENTERED. REAL IMPACT.

PROMISES KEPT
978-0-8024-2895-0

PREDICTING JESUS
978-0-8024-2511-9

AN UNEXPECTED
REVIVAL
978-0-8024-2500-3

THE GODLY KINGS OF
JUDAH
978-0-8024-2174-6

BEFORE THE THRONE
978-0-8024-2378-8

THE EXTRAORDINARY
POWER OF PRAISE
978-0-8024-2009-1

SUMMONED
978-0-8024-2169-2

A GREAT CLOUD OF
WITNESSES
978-0-8024-2107-4

Explore our Bible studies at
moodypublisherswomen.com

Also available as eBooks